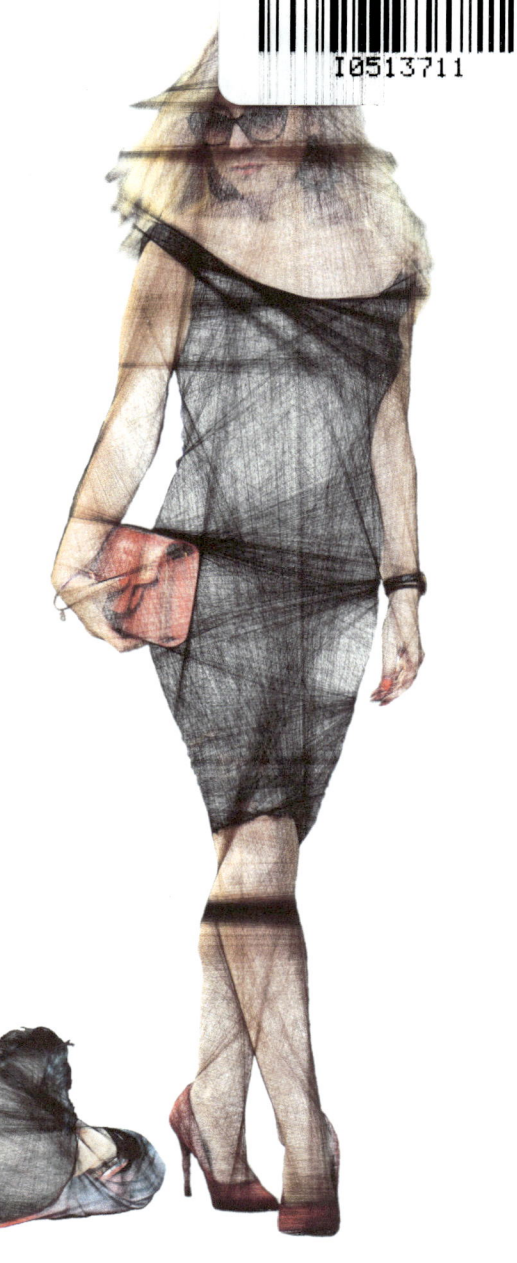

MEN AND WOMEN
VOLUME ONE

PASQUALE GAMBARELLI

Copyright © Pasquale Gambarelli

All rights reserved, which includes the right to reproduce this book or portions thereof in any form whatsoever.

Independently published
Publication date: September 14, 2020

For information contact:
MenAndWomen0920@gmail.com

This book is dedicated to those who, while loving art and graphics
have given up expressing themselves because they believe they
do not possess the relevant technical skills.
To make this book I used a ten-year-old computer
and free programs like Gimp that are commonly available.
If I have succeeded you can succeed too but you will never know if
you do not try and put aside your fears.

TABLE OF CONTENTS

Regrets..2

Letting go...4

Is this FACEBOOK?...6

Out loud...8

The world in a box...10

The eye..12

The flight..14

Wind blow..16

Social Media..18

Dreaming...20

Life goes on...22

The sculptor...24

Gossip...26

Hunting territory...28

Going away...30

The proposal...32

Loneliness...34

End of a love...36

Meeting...38

The border..40

Window with blue view..42

Window with purple view...44

Window with red view..46

The road..48

Farewell..50

Going away..52

Past, present and future..54

The kiss...56

The kiss - Picture on the left...59

The kiss - Picture in the middle..60

The kiss - Picture on the right...61

The kiss – A man, a woman..62

The kiss - The couple..63

INTRODUCTION

This book is a personal experiment that I did to express my love for painting, photography and the graphic arts in general.

This love was born when, at the age of about 14, I read an article by Giulio Carlo Argan about a painting depicting the Crucifixion set in a medieval city.

The article struck me because Argan described the work with a narrative technique that used the story through a journey within the painting.

Argan began the journey from the top of the Cross and then continued down to the dice players at the foot of the Cross who were playing the clothes of Jesus.

The Cross with the players was at the crossroads of a road so Argan continued his journey through the road behind the Cross.

Throughout this journey Argan never ceased to go into the details, into the lives of those human beings and conveyed to me the importance of the details in giving value to the overall picture.

I learned that you can never appreciate the general picture if you don't have the courage to dive into the details and the strength to walk away from it to return to the general picture and then dive into another detail and go up again.

It will be this continuous coming and going that will give value and depth to your interpretation of what you have in front of you.

I soon realized that I would need a good guide and time, a lot of time.

I could have found the guide, but time was my sword of Damocles.

After all, 14 years live only once in a lifetime.

I was content to do some gurgling from time to time and to observe, read, study those works on which I could lay my eyes going in search of those details that gave value to the general picture and that story that gave free rein to my imagination.

At about 17 years old, in one of my readings, I came across another article where there was a photo of André Kertész taken during a reportage in Japan.

It was a simple black and white photo of a Japanese garden with a boulder in the center surrounded by waves drawn in gravel.

The author of the writing said that that garden, that photo represented the Japanese concept of Zen.

With my great wonder I learned that images can evoke even particularly complicated things such as concepts, sensations, moods.

I couldn't help but notice the cleanliness, the lines, the warm color of that black and white photo.

It was because of that photo that, as soon as I had the chance, I bought myself an Olympus OM 10 and started taking pictures playing to do so much experimental research.

Only a few years later, looking at photographs contained in the collection of the Select Foundation referring to the Great Masters of the '50s, '60s and' 70s and exhibited at Forte Belvedere in Florence, I realized the real greatness of Kertész and the value of the photographs of the Great Masters exhibited there.

Unfortunately Kertész, in his day, was not fully understood but suffice it to say that Henri Cartier-Bresson had to say that all photographers of his generation owed something to Kertész.

Even today, watching movies or news I find myself watching some of Kertész's shots and I wonder if the author of that movie or news knows his name.

In that exhibition, in addition to the photos of Kertész, I discovered other great masters and was impressed by the works of Ernst Haas.

The black and white was beautiful but the colour was pure colour.

His photos were gorgeous.

They expressed a poetry inexpressible in words, something common to all Greats, but at the same time they vibrated with music.

A music that, although with different shades, I found in other great ones.

It was pure art as far as I was concerned.

I was looking for some Italian photographer who could be approached by these giants.

After so much searching I finally managed to discover Mario Giacomelli.

Giacomelli was a poet with a sweet, romantic and I dare say nostalgic vision of life.

His photos express a calm, quiet, intimate music that has fascinated me since the first time I saw them.

Giacomelli was a true Poet who expressed himself in an apparently simple way.

If you can tear the veil of this appearance you will discover an extremely cultured, refined, sought after Poet with a boundless love for the human being.

His black and white photos are incredible.

Never met or seen another Italian at his level.

In the mid 80's the first computers began to appear and I jumped headlong in an attempt to figure out what they were capable of, but not before I discovered René François Ghislain Magritte, Maurits Cornelis Escher and many others.

When I resigned I wanted to make an exhibition of some of my photographs but the prints were painful.

In 1994 the professional workshops were closing one after the other because the village photographers were equipping themselves with equipment that automatically developed and printed the photographs.

The problem is that a machine, however good it may be, cannot replace the experience, the analytical capacity of the eye of a human being who has practiced for several years becoming an Expert.

Not yet at least.

The machine is led to commit, for limits due to the competence of those who built it and the technological resources used, completely trivial, coarse and sometimes gruesome errors.

These workshops from home were no different, but people continued to pay for horrible prints.

I understood that people do not know how to recognize quality and that the era of the negative was over.

Why am I saying all this?

Because in this work I wanted to build my own exhibition using everything I learned and that made me who I am.

Since there are some sites that have free photographic images with licenses that allow or even invite you to edit such photos, I decided to use the photos that recur in these sites trying to give light to photographers who share their work with others for free and who, much more often than not, are really very good at it.

Obviously, for each of the photos I used, I took the trouble to note down the site from which I downloaded the image and its date with the name of the Author.

Why did I do this?

Because I have noticed that, sometimes, some photos magically disappear from the site and then a copyright infringement request arrives.

Unfortunately, correctness is not within everyone's reach.

In order to create my compositions I used several images from which I extrapolated the details that interested me.

These details were modified with pictorial techniques that I thought were appropriate for what I wanted to express through the use of free programs easily available on the Internet like Gimp.

In many cases even the Authors of the photos would not be able to recognize their photos.

I used these photos and the programs I had available as colours on a painter's palette, mixing them together to achieve the desired effect.

This meant that, in the end, I always had to work manually using the brushes and other tools that Gimp gave me to modify, correct and finish the composition.

I don't know Gimp very well as I have only been using it for a couple of months but I can only be grateful to its Authors for the resource they have made available to me.

Unfortunately, the size of this book does not allow an adequate view of the work I have included in it, so I have made the decision to start the images from the first available even page, instead of the odd one as usual, so as to flank the reproduction of the general view (on the left) with the reproduction of a detail in scale 1 : 1 of a magnification of the work increased to 90 centimetres (on the right).

The reason is dictated by the fact that the images in this book, in order to be fully enjoyed, should be reproduced at about 90 - 100 centimetres.

To enlarge this detail, I took the longest dimension of the image, the horizontal one, which is about 38.10 centimetres, and enlarged it to 90.00 centimetres.

From the magnification obtained in this way I cut out a detail with the largest size equal to 18.10 centimetres because the horizontal dimension of the image on this book is 18.10 centimetres.

In this way it is possible to observe details that cannot be captured in the overall view.

The only exception is the last image in which, given its relative complexity, I wanted to insert two details and an image dedicated to each element of the composition.

Since there are also images of a man and a woman, I wanted to combine these two elements in a single image to play with them a little bit and observe the relative effect.

I hope that the work can be considered original and can find the appreciation of those who will have the strength, time and courage to look at these images.

Below is a list of the sites and photographers who have helped me, with their work, to carry on this effort.

It seems quite obvious to me that there are some Authors of whom I have used more than one photo but their name is reported only once so as not to give the reader false indications.

The fact that I have used more photos of one Author than another does not mean that the Author with more photos is better.

What I can say is that I was impressed by the overall quality of women's work.

Moreover, I did not link the names of the Authors who contributed to a certain composition with the composition itself.

The consideration that prompted me to make this choice is due to the fact that, if anyone would like to get to know these Authors better, it would be appropriate to go and see their original photos on the relevant sites.

I think you would be amazed at the ability and skill of some of them.

To all of them my heartfelt thanks in the hope that I have not forgotten any of them.

AUTHORS OF THE PHOTOS USED

PEXELS	PIXABAY	UNSPLASH
Adrien Olichon	2081671	Guillaume Meurice
Alex Fu	Anastasia Gepp	Ryan Moreno
Alexander Krivitskiy	angelinaschneegans	
Andrea Piacquadio	Anna_Bella	
Bruno Thethe	Awais Mughal	
cottonbro	Barbora Franzová	
Daria Shevtsova	Bernd Bitzer	
Demeter Attila	Christo Anestev	

FransA	Dina Dee
Godisable Jacob	Jerzy Górecki
Jacub Gomez	johnpotter
Jessica Lewis	Khusen Rustamov
JT Kim	My pictures are CC0. When doing composings
Just Name	Patrick Pascal Schauß
Kaique Rocha	Paul Barlow
Marcos Miranda	Sarah Richter
mentadgt	seagul
Nicholas Swatz	Silviu Costin Iancu
Olya Kobruseva	StockSnap
picjumbo.com	Wokandapix
Pille Kirsi	Wolfgang Eckert
Radu Florin	
Rene Asmussen	
Vera Arsic	
Wellington Cunha	

GOOD SIGHT

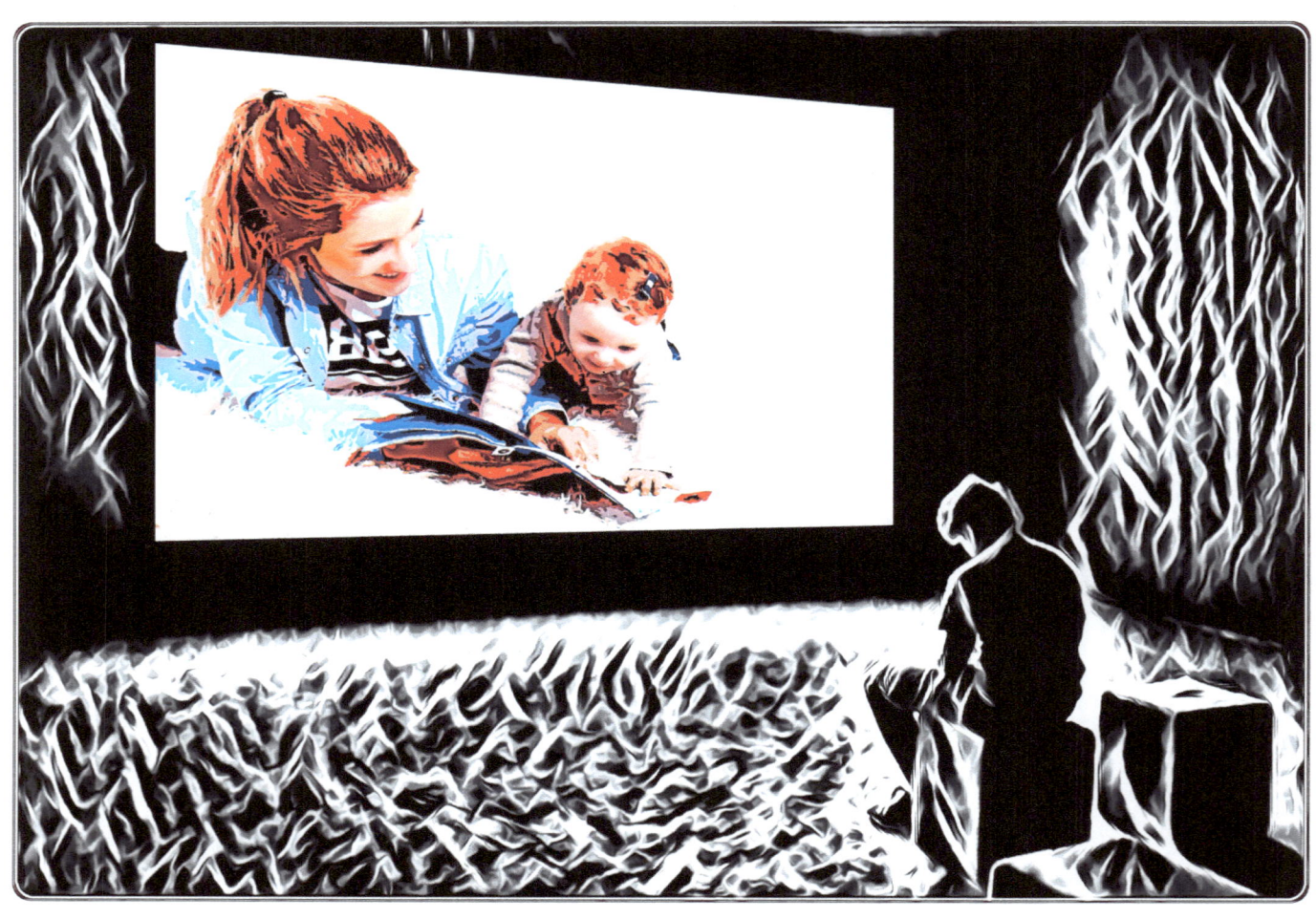

Regrets

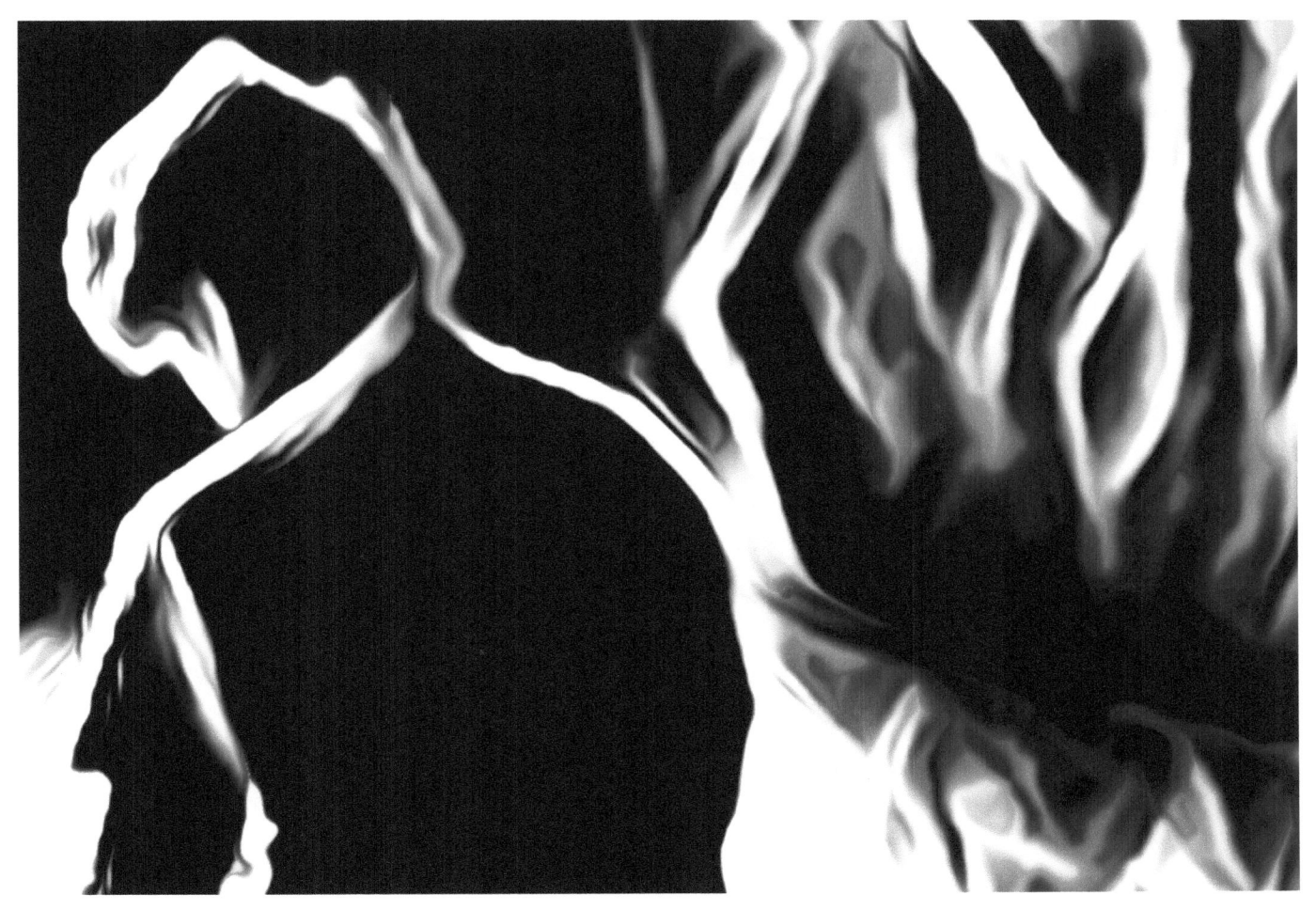

Regrets - Detail

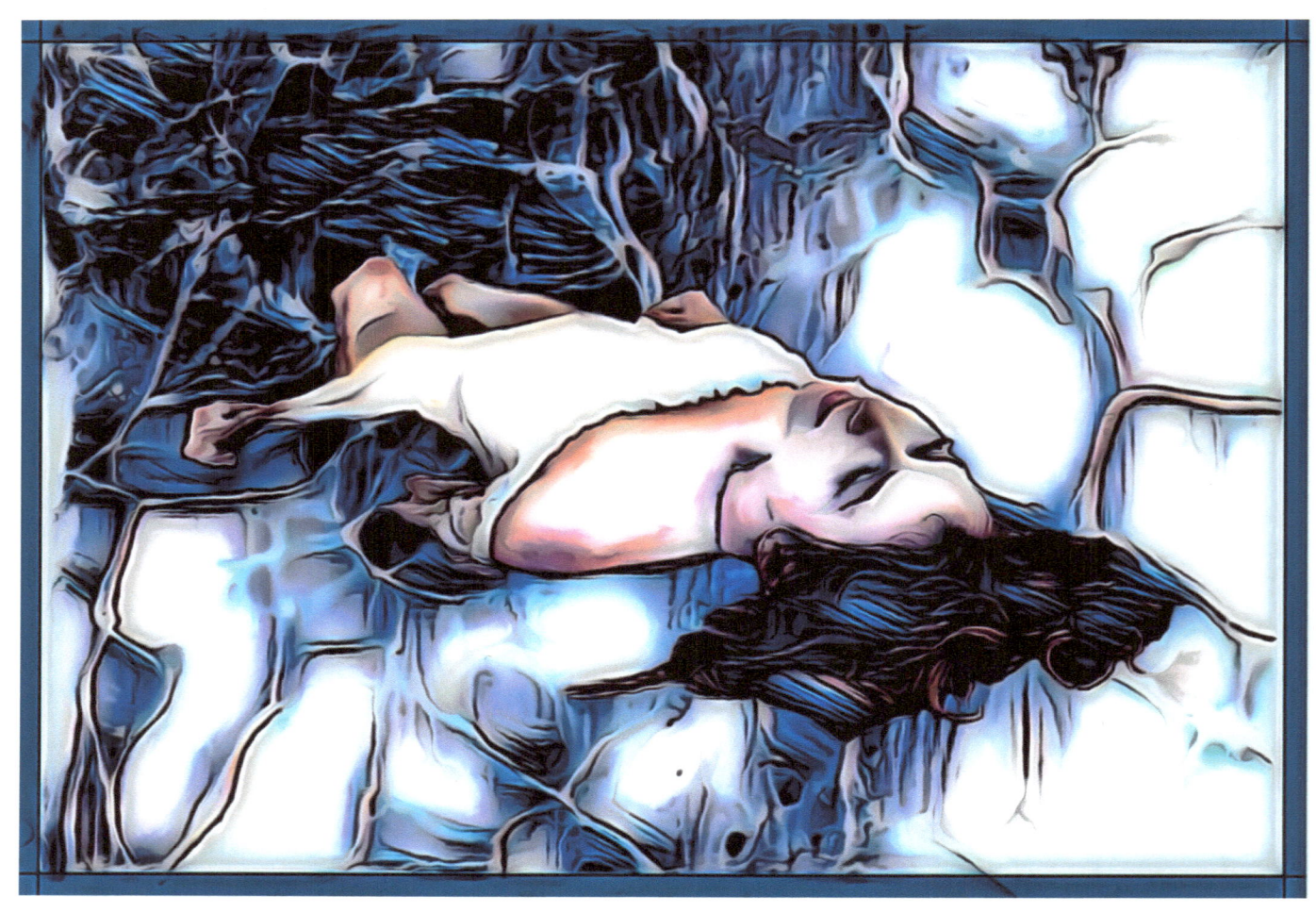

Letting go

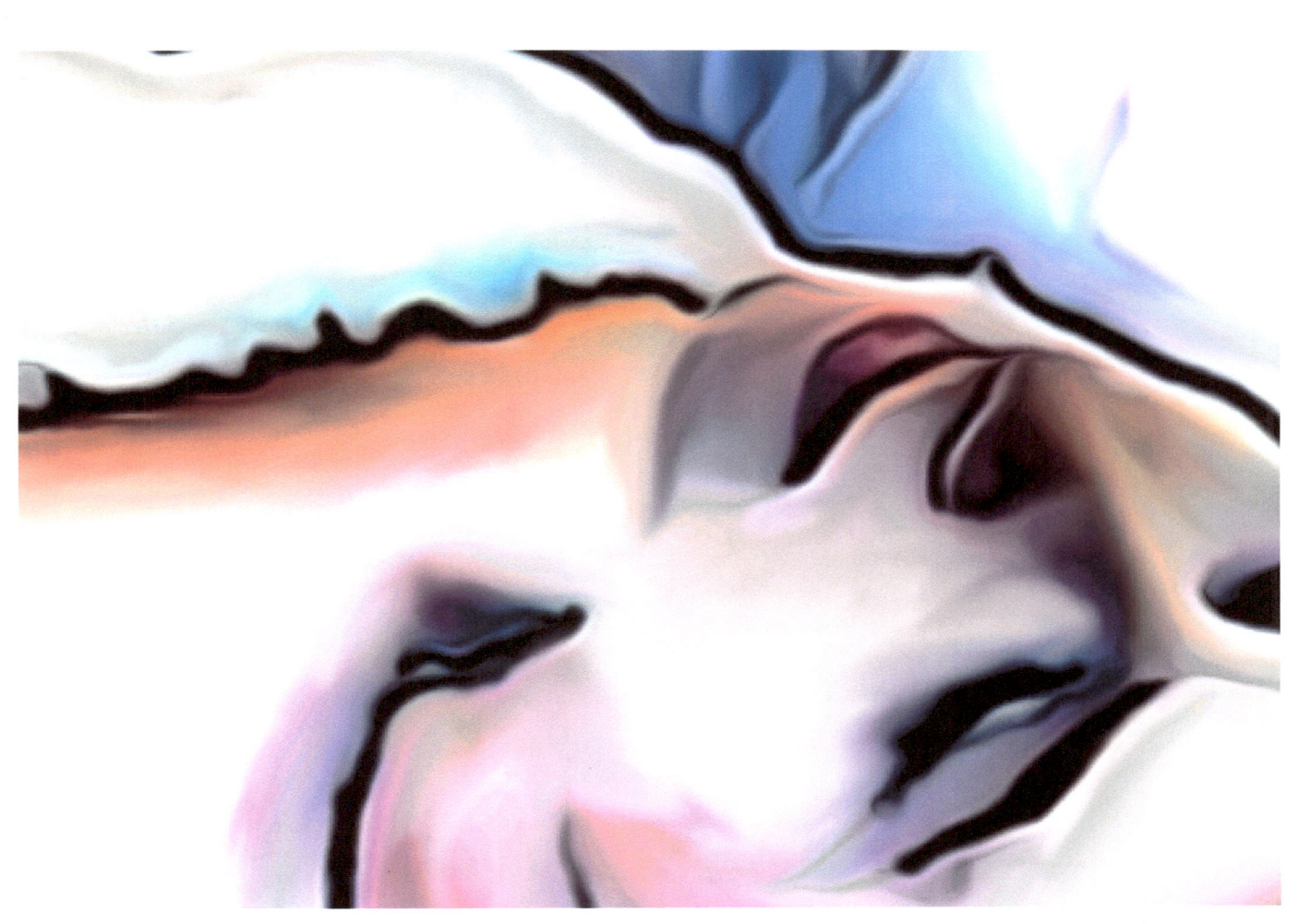

Letting go - detail

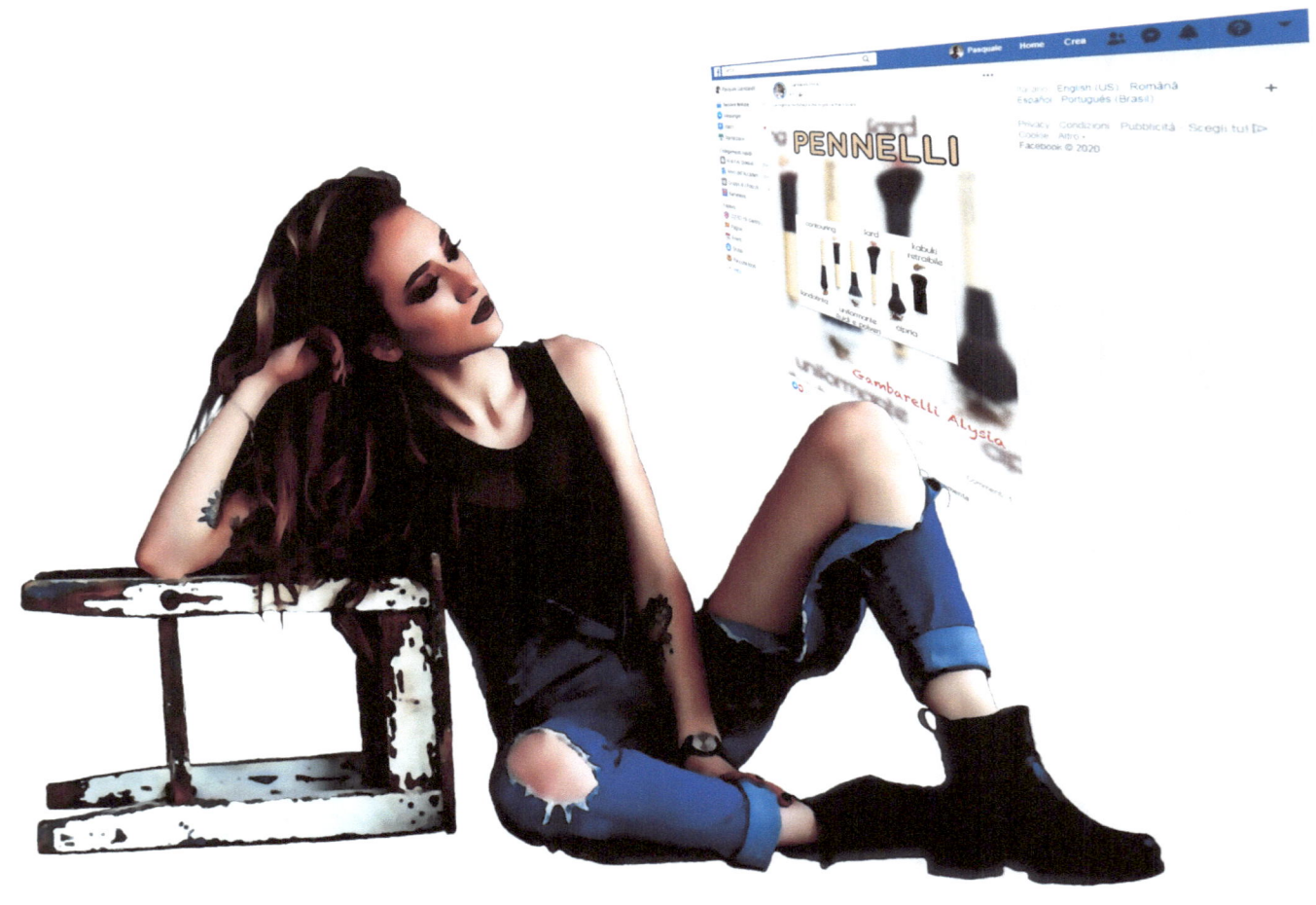

Is this FACEBOOK?

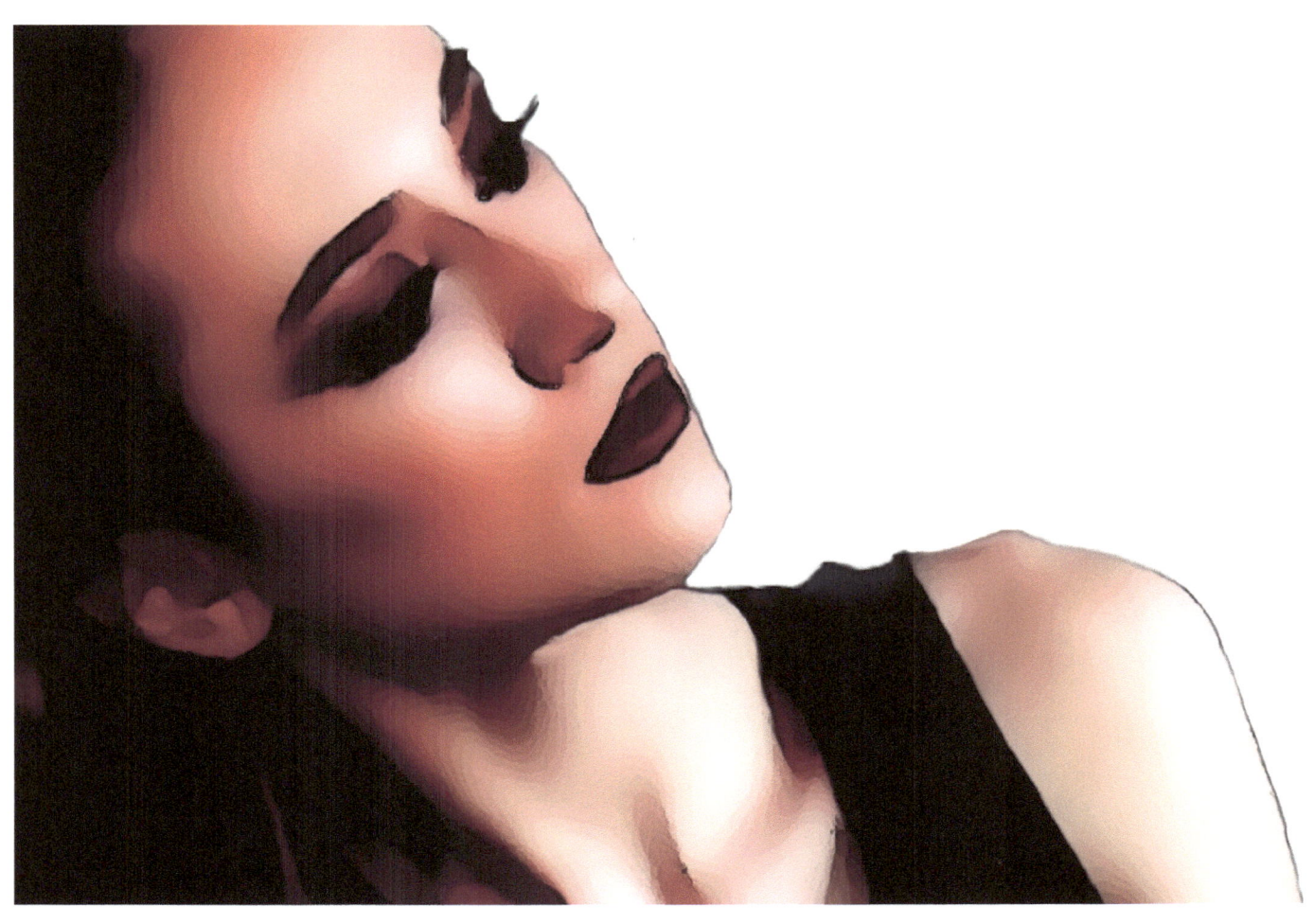

Is this FACEBOOK? - Detail

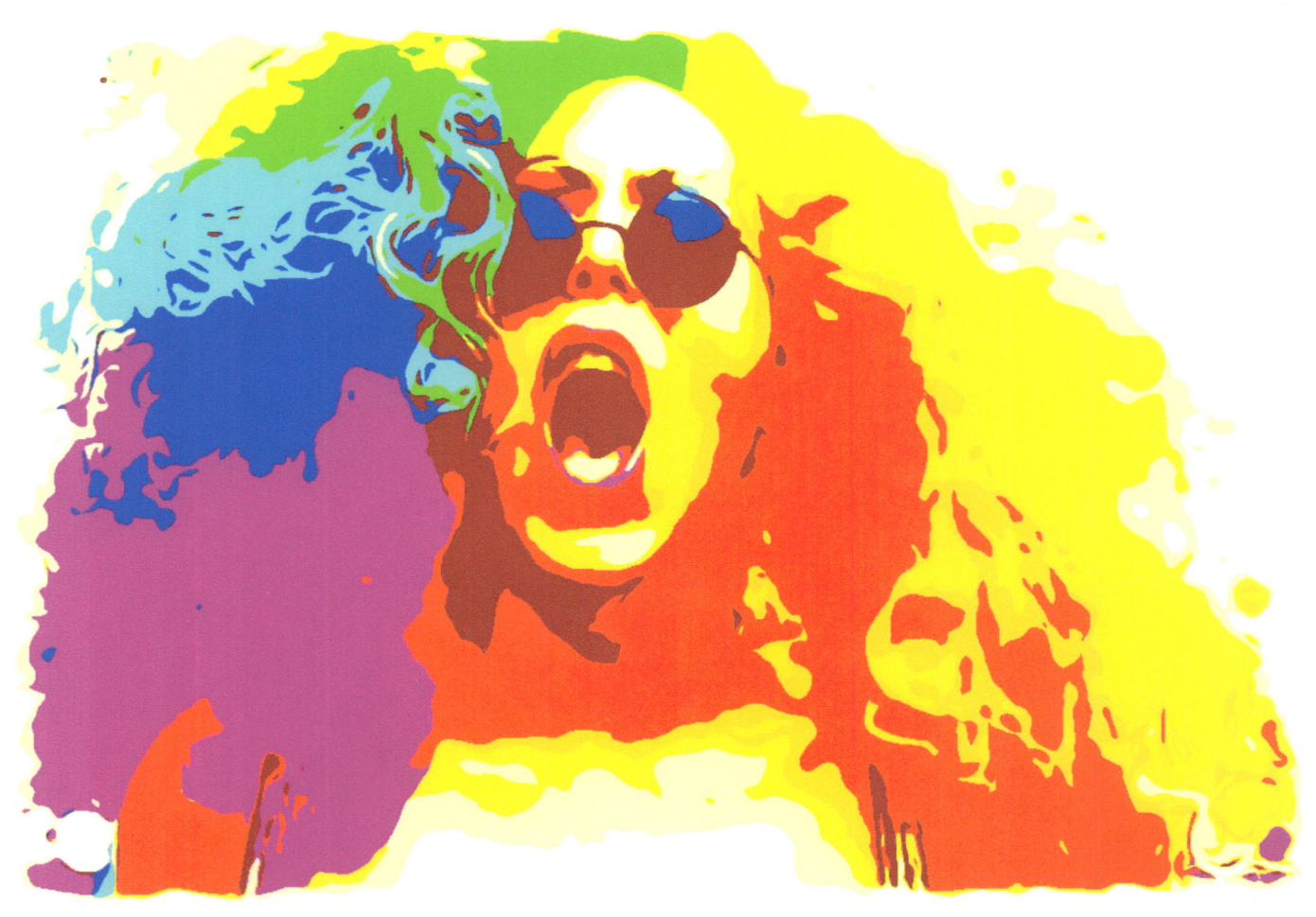

Out loud

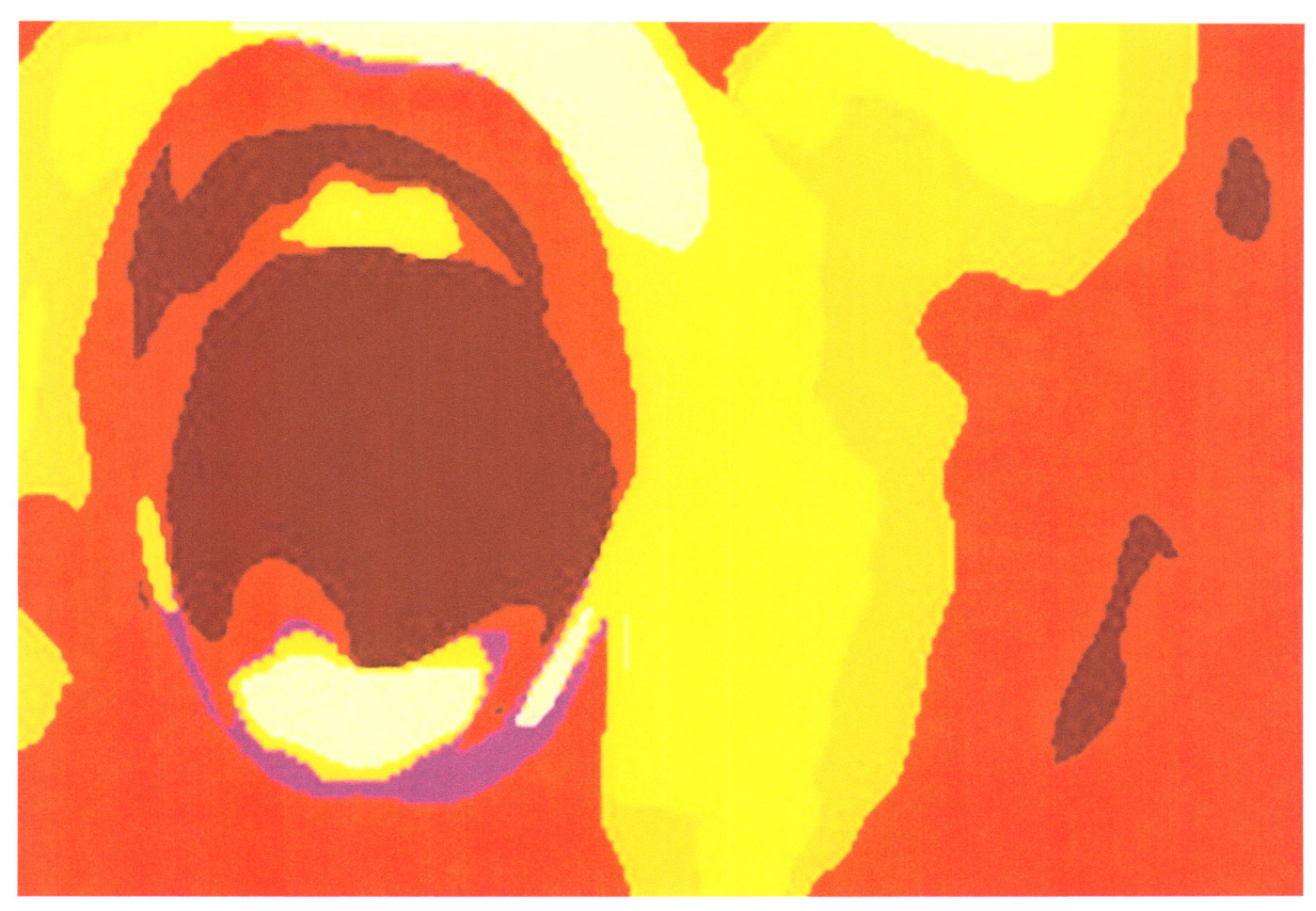

Out loud - Detail

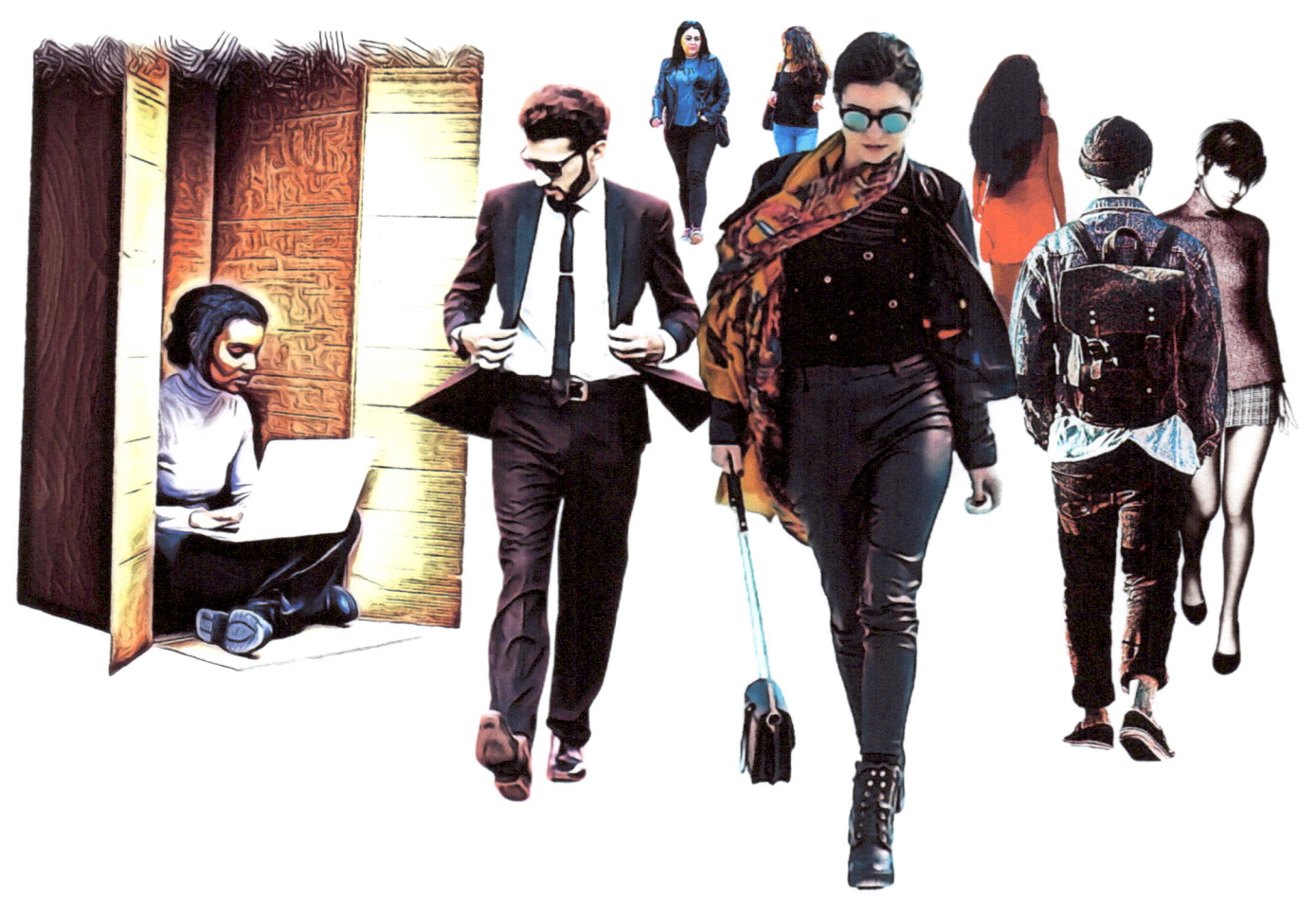

The world in a box

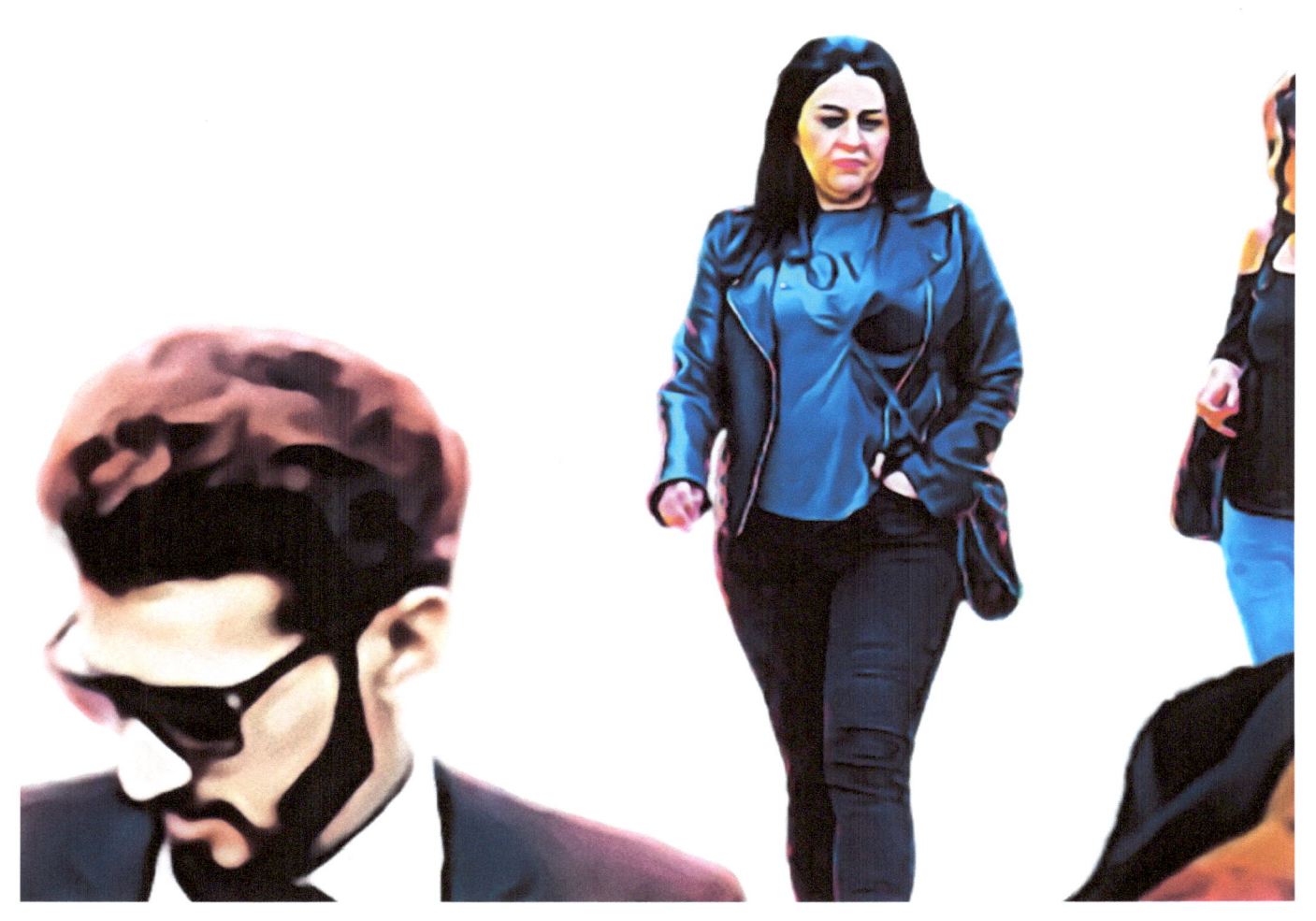

The world in a box - Detail

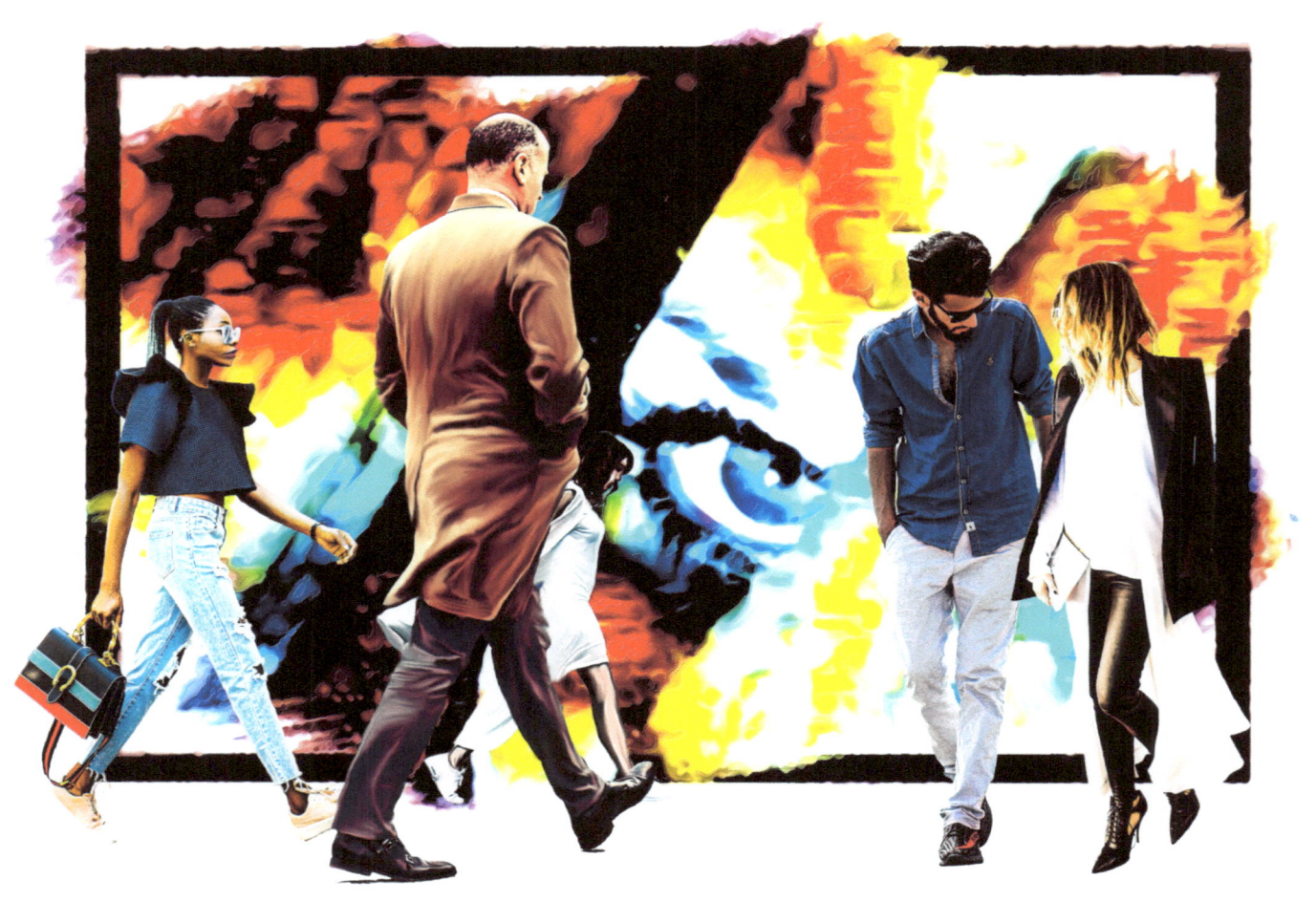

The eye

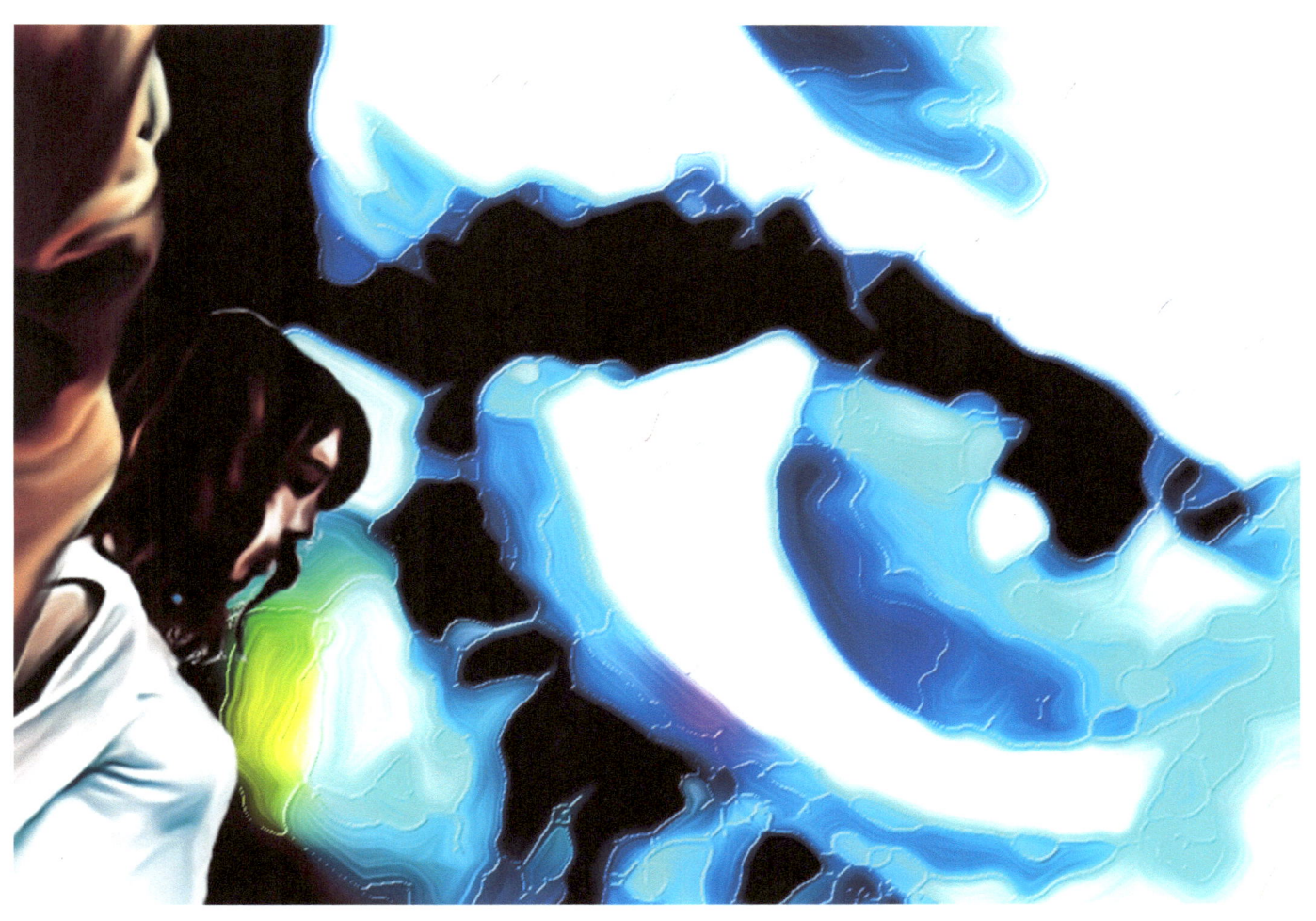

The eye - Detail

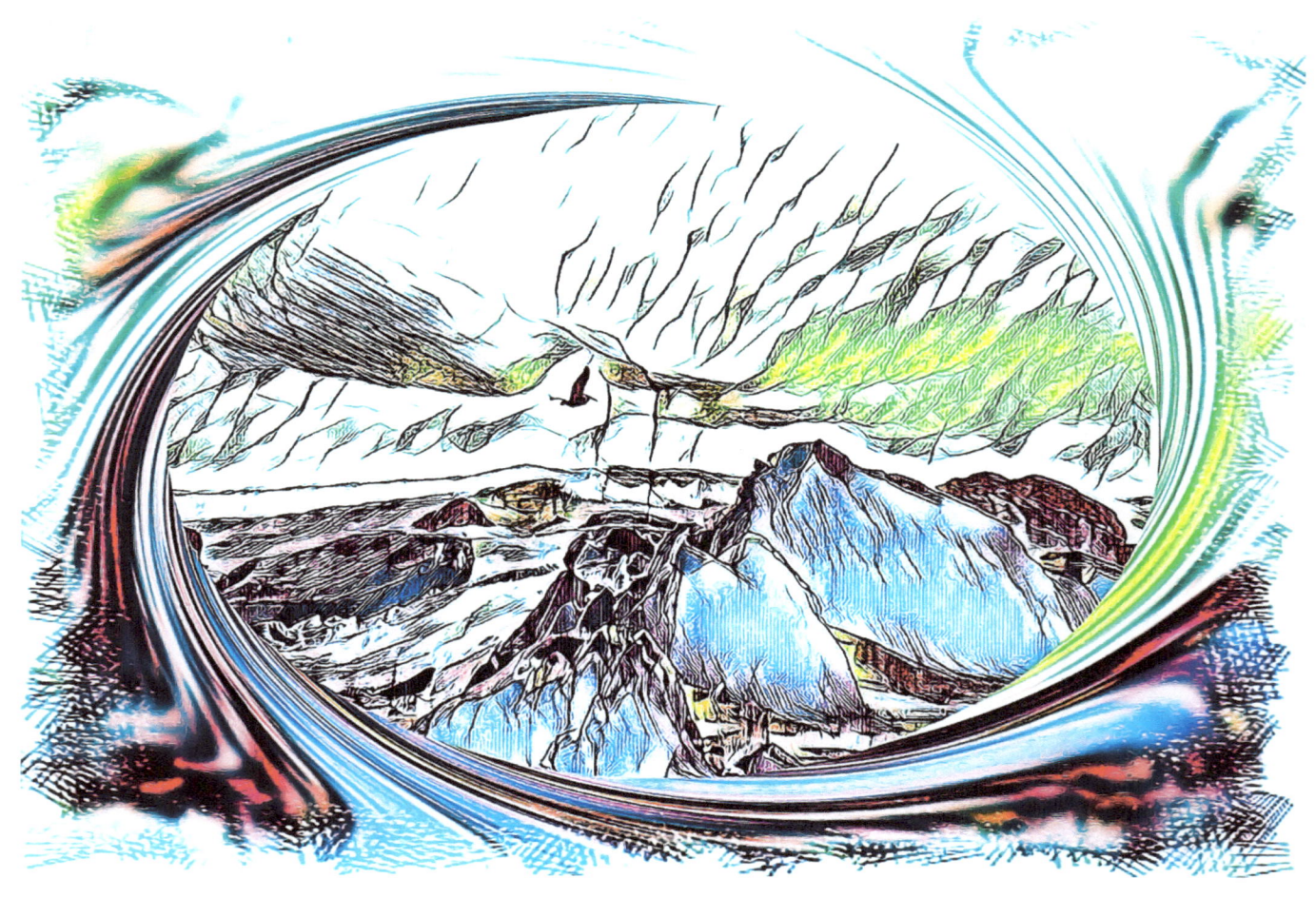

The flight

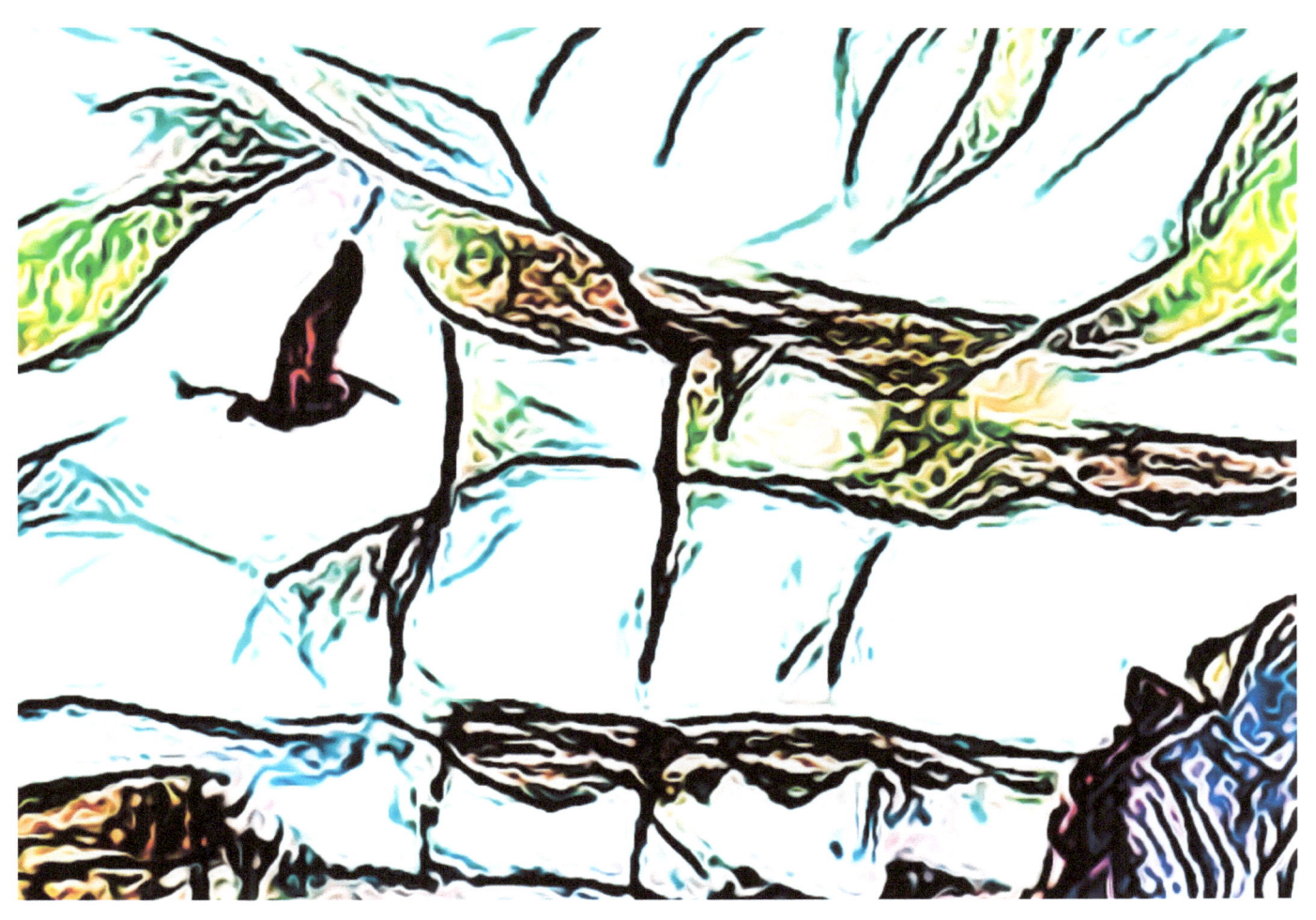

The flight - Detail

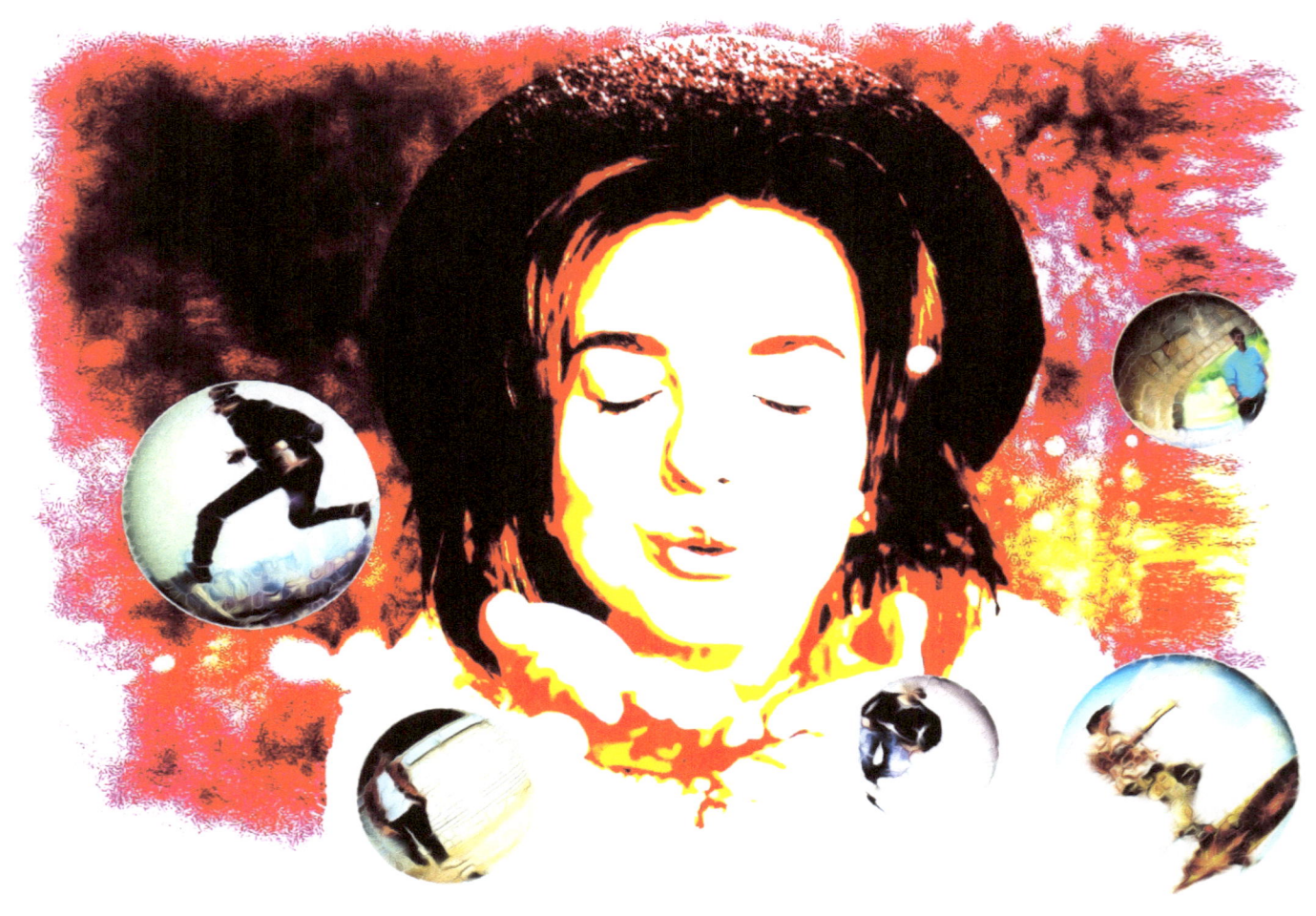

Wind blow

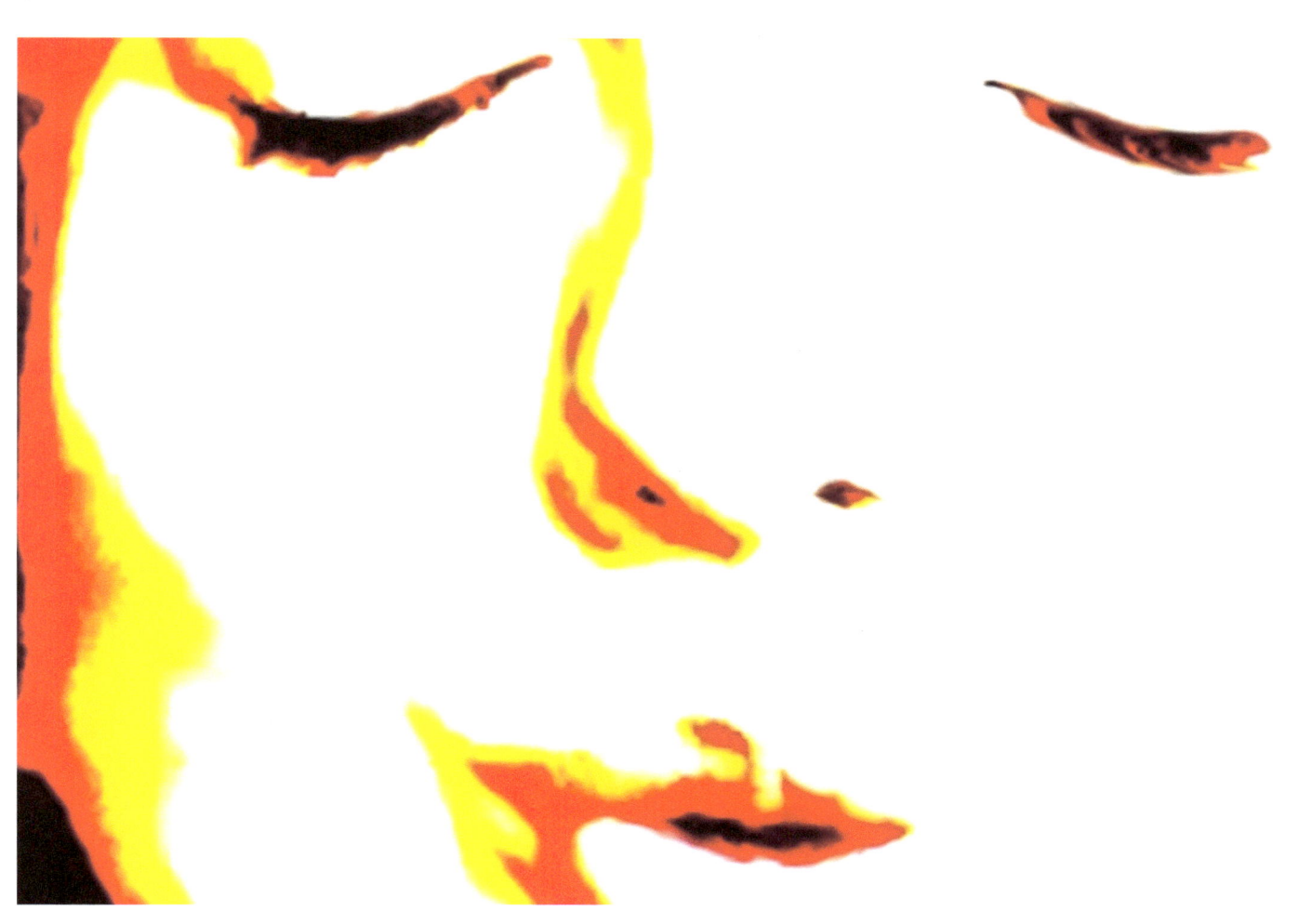

Wind blow - detail

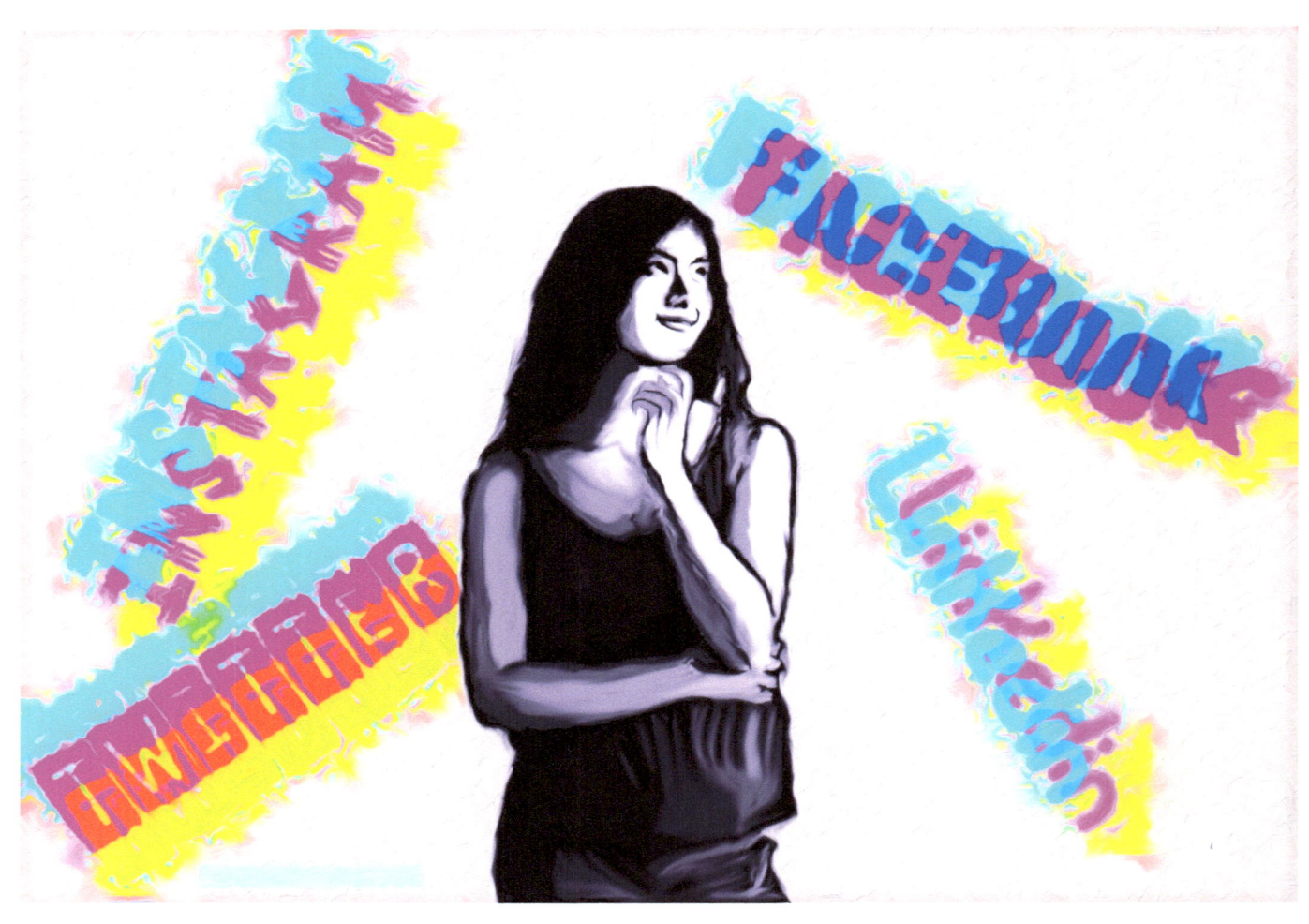

Social Media

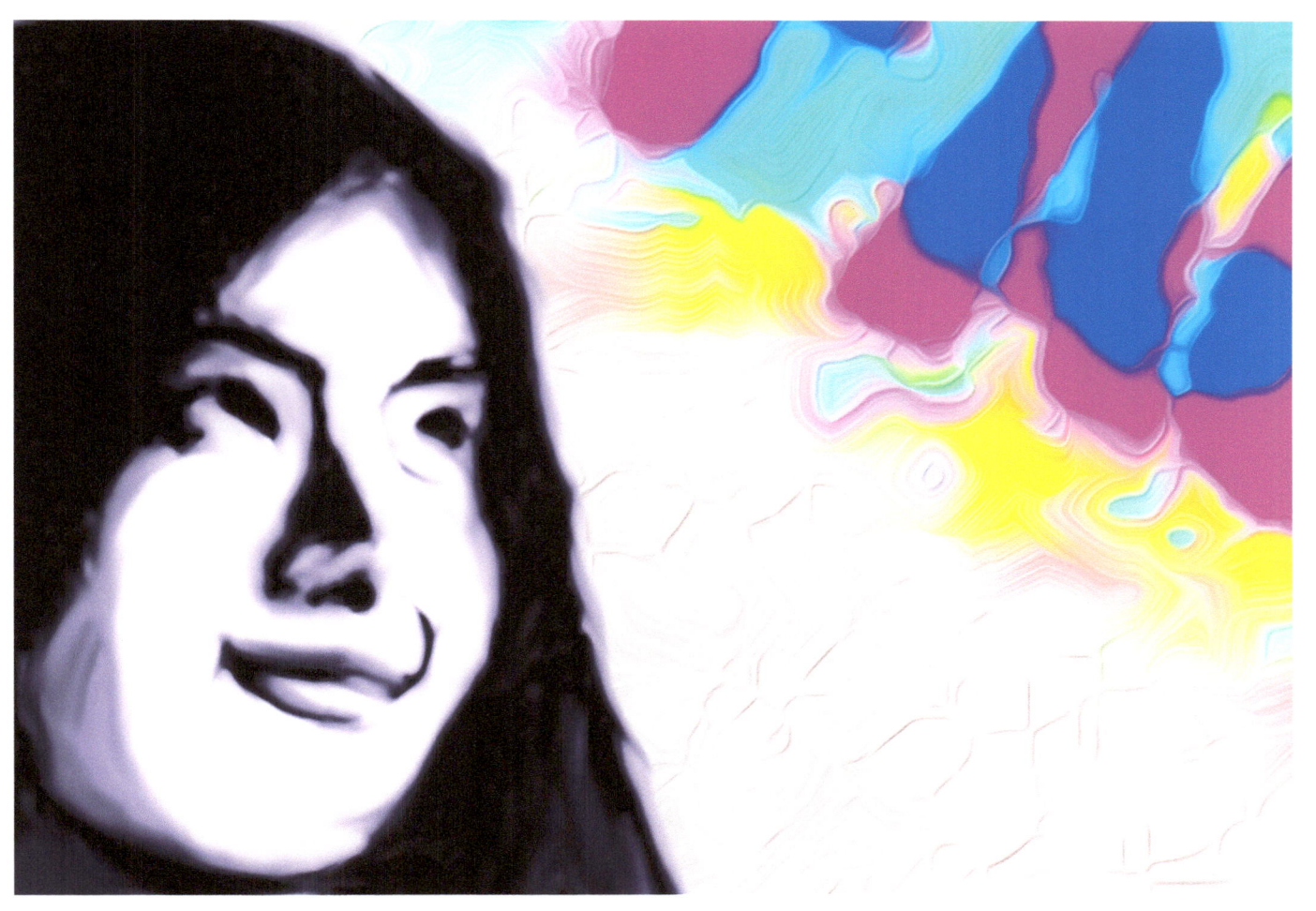

Social Media - Detail

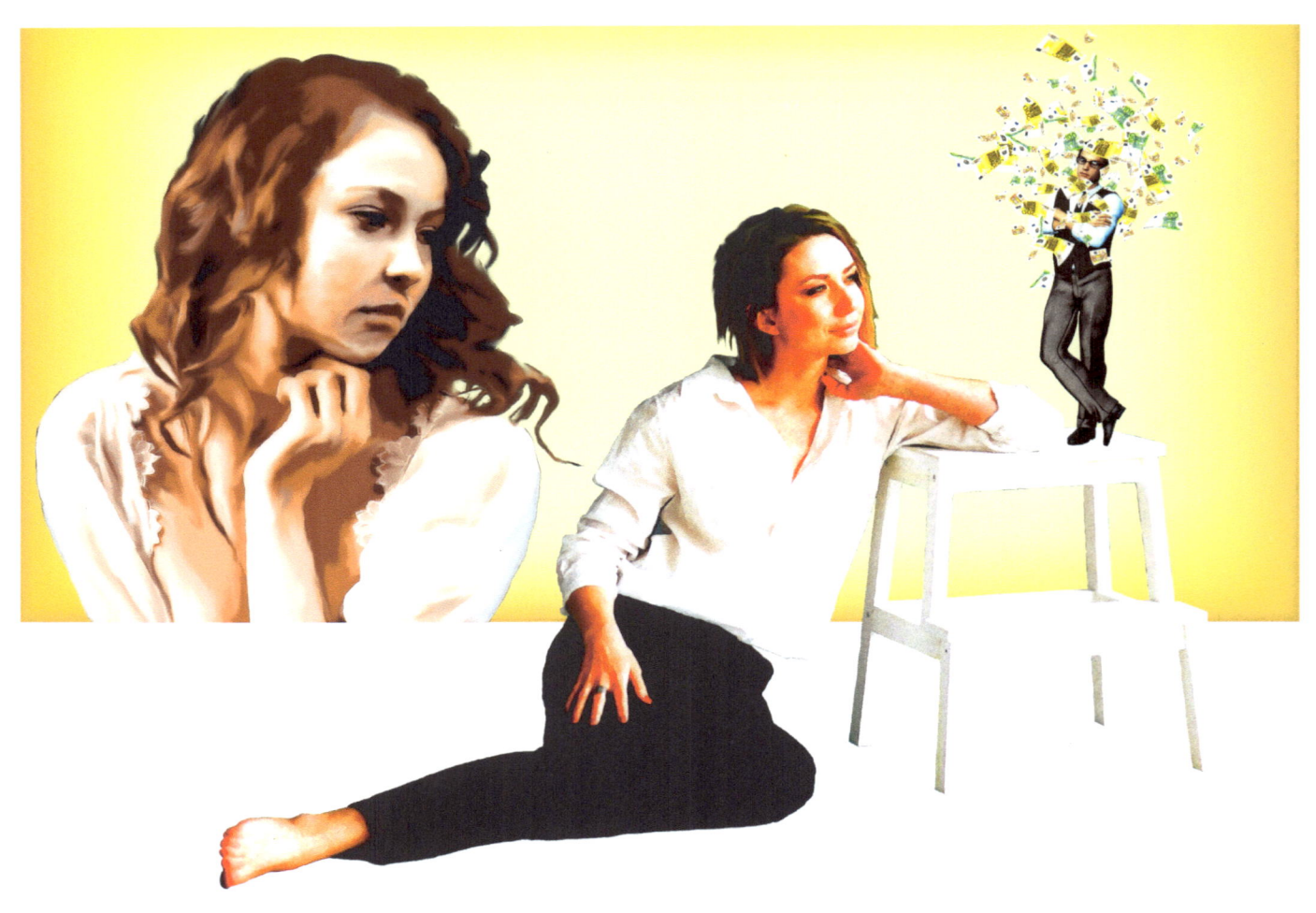

Dreaming

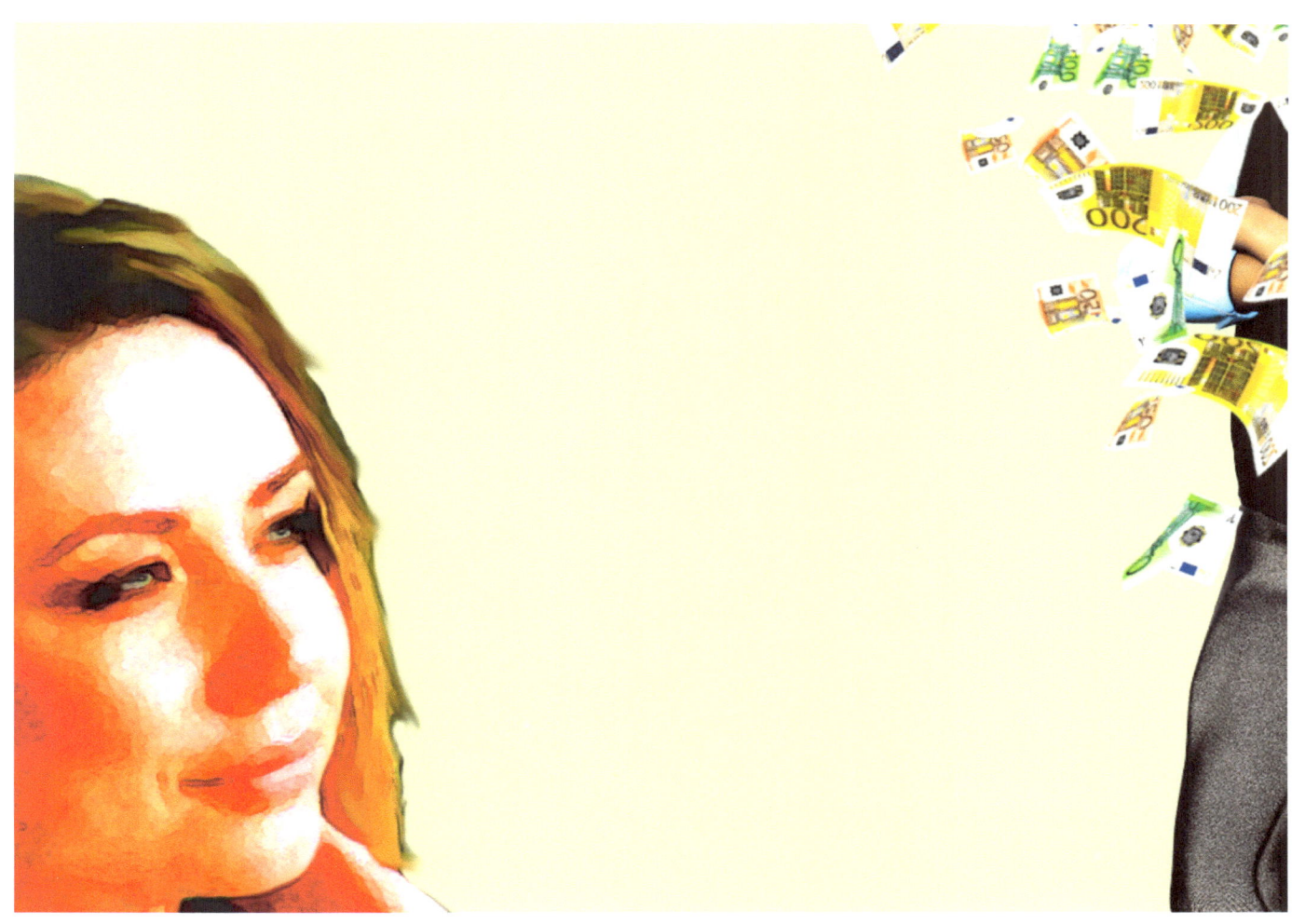

Dreaming - Detail

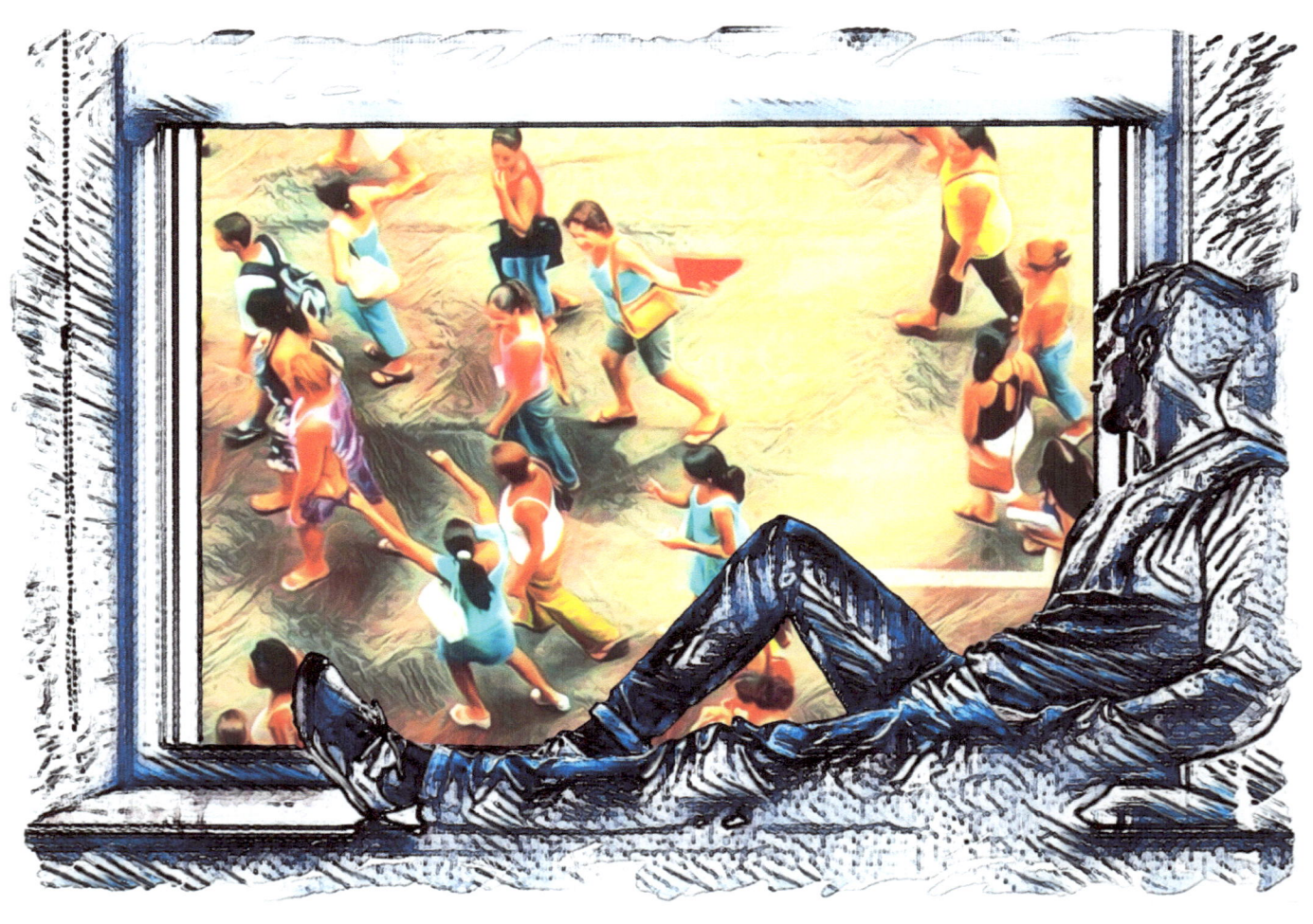

Life goes on

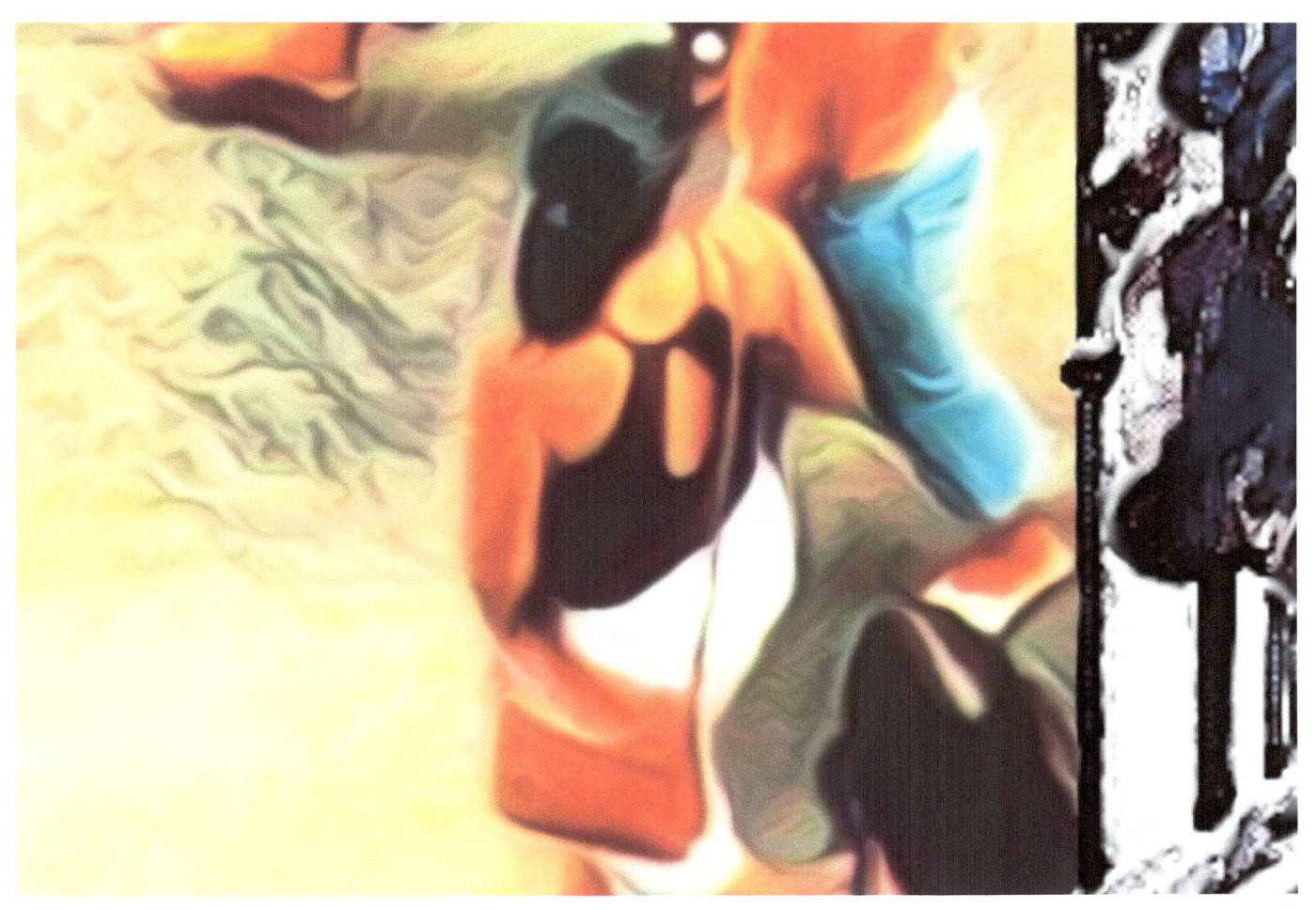

Life goes on - Detail

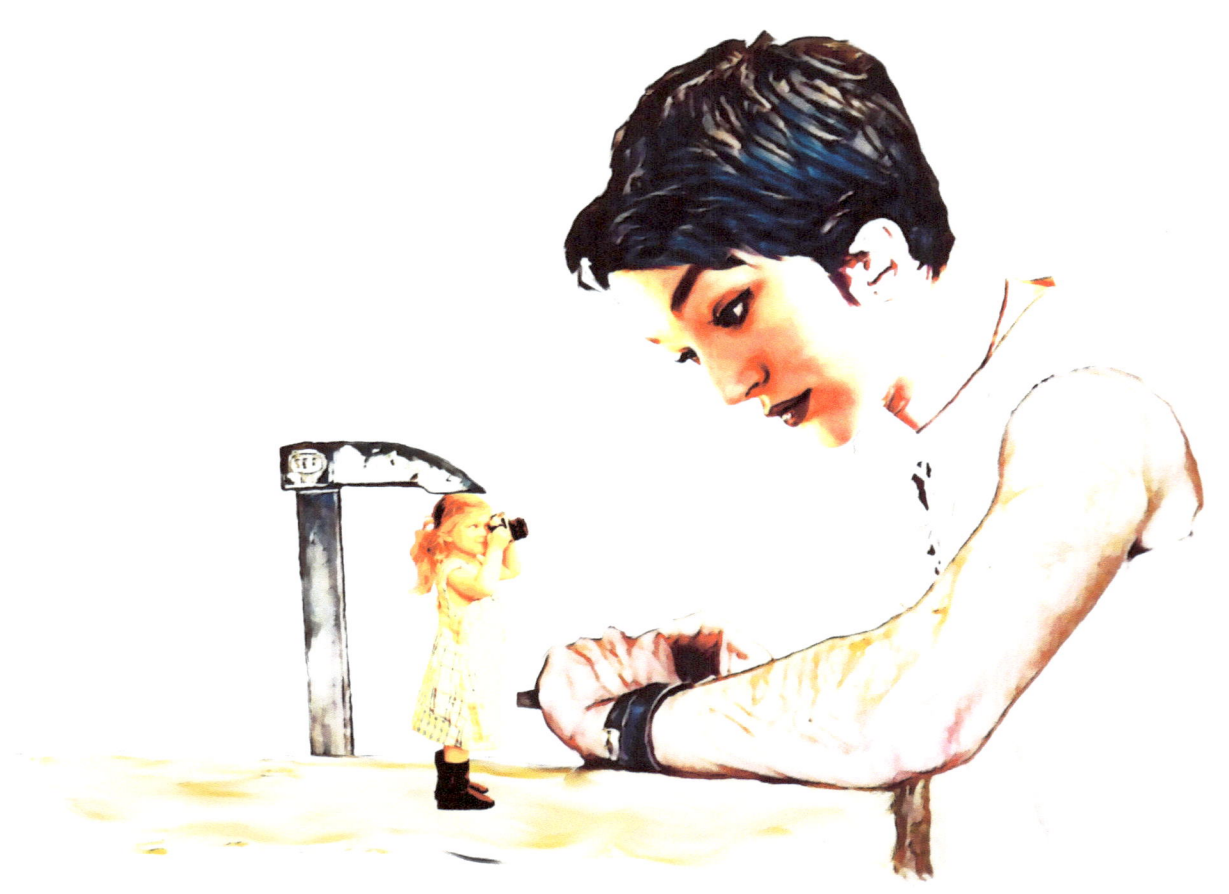

The sculptor

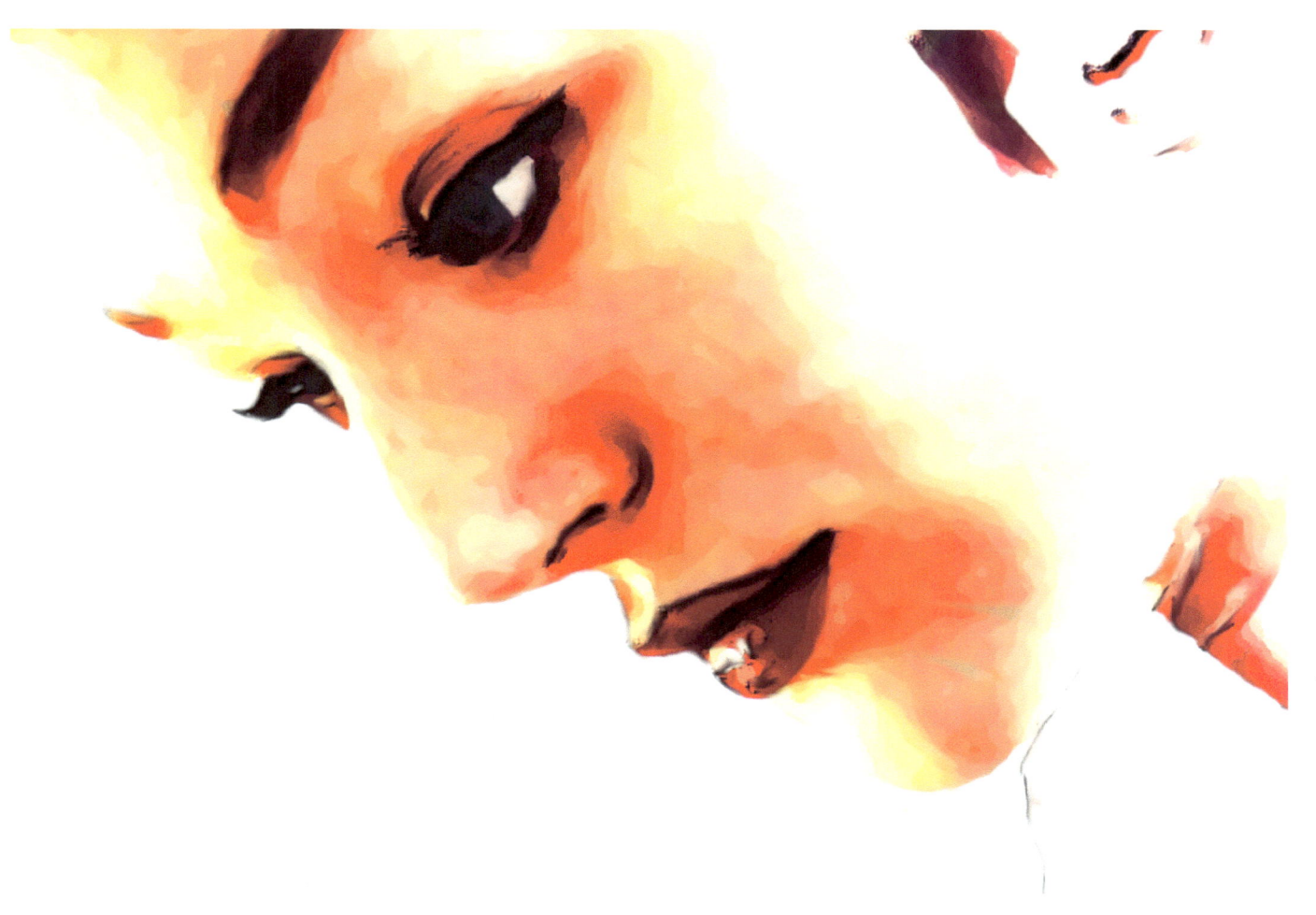

The sculptor - Detail

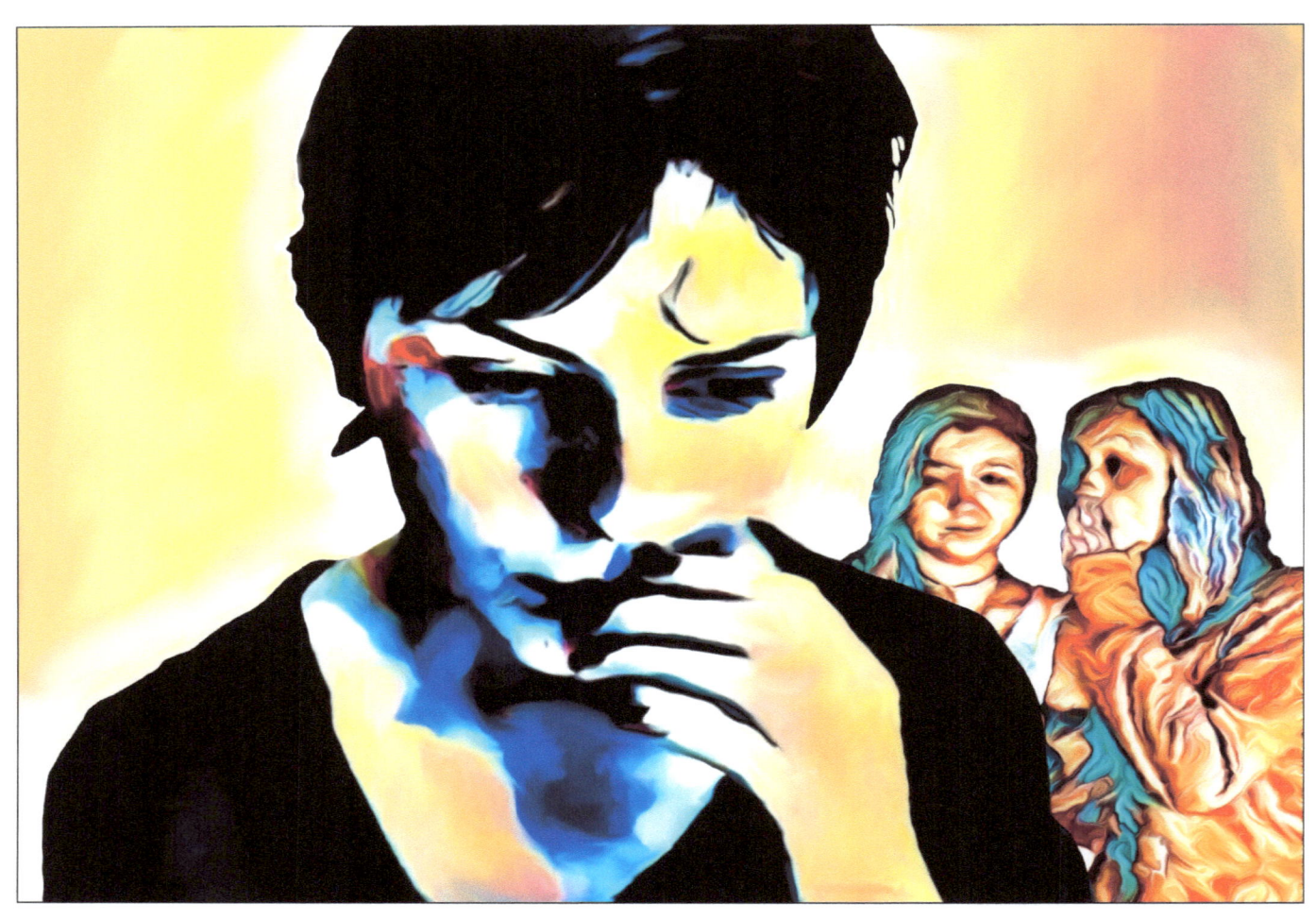

Gossip

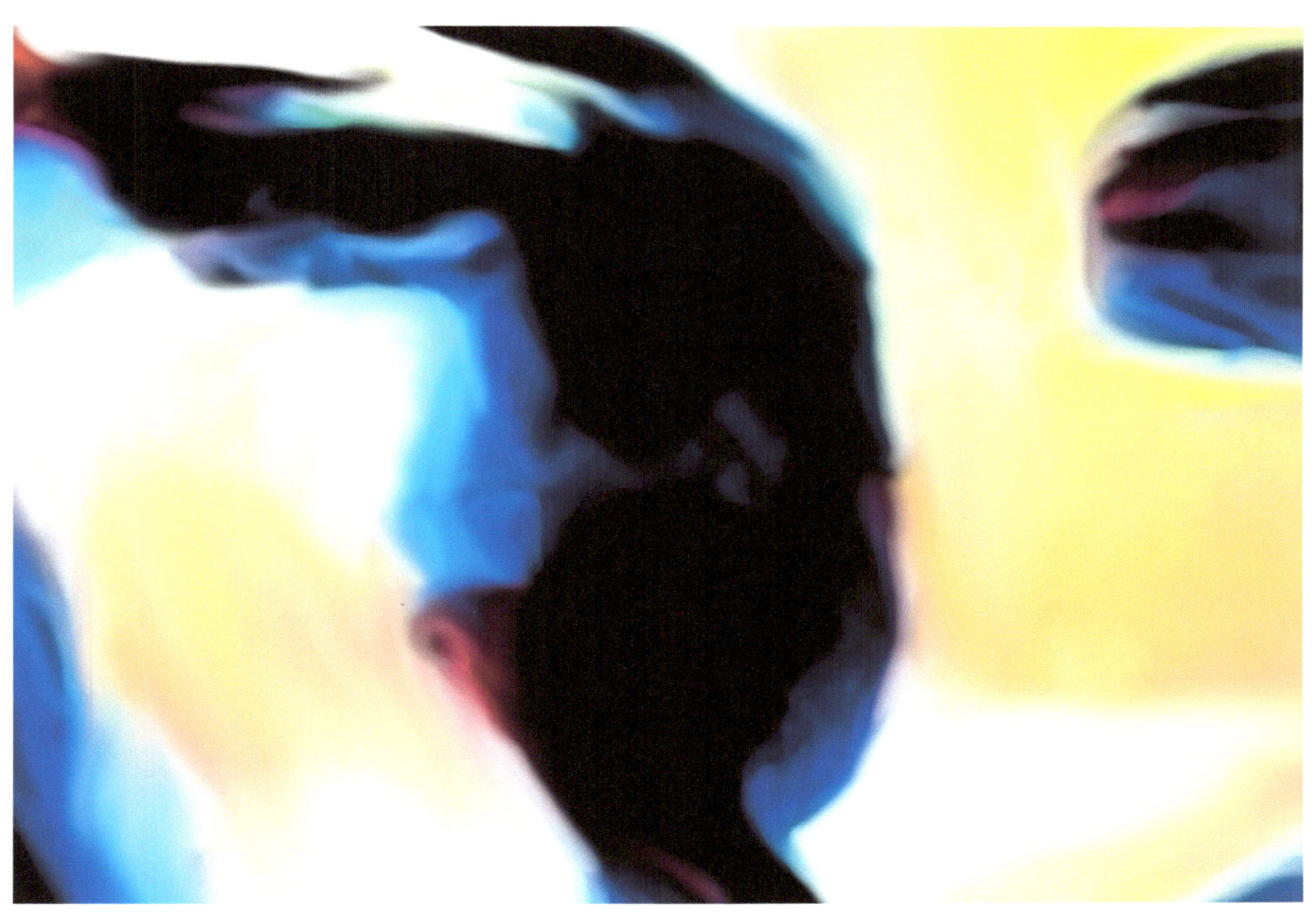

Gossip - Detail

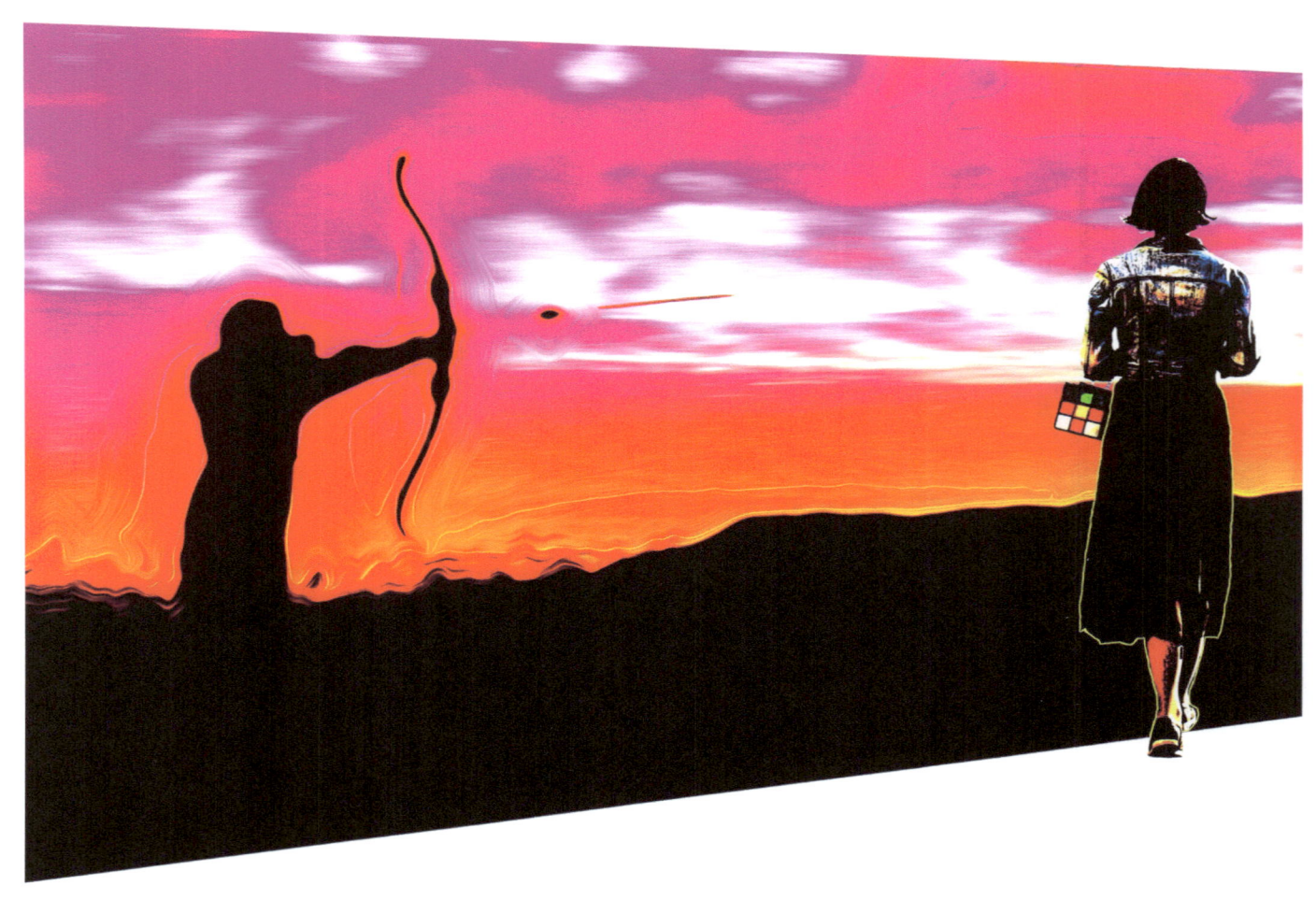

Hunting territory

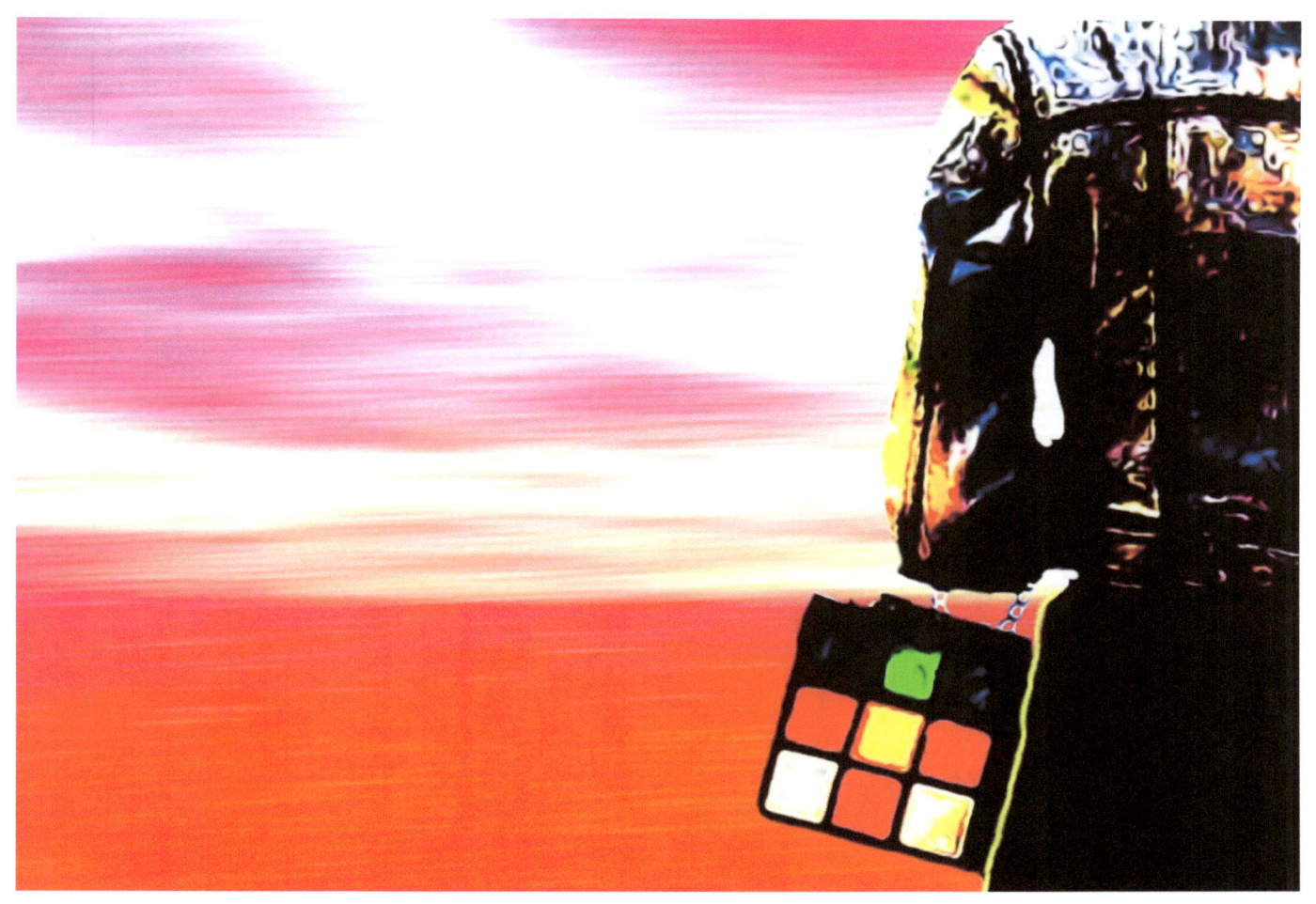

Hunting territory - Detail

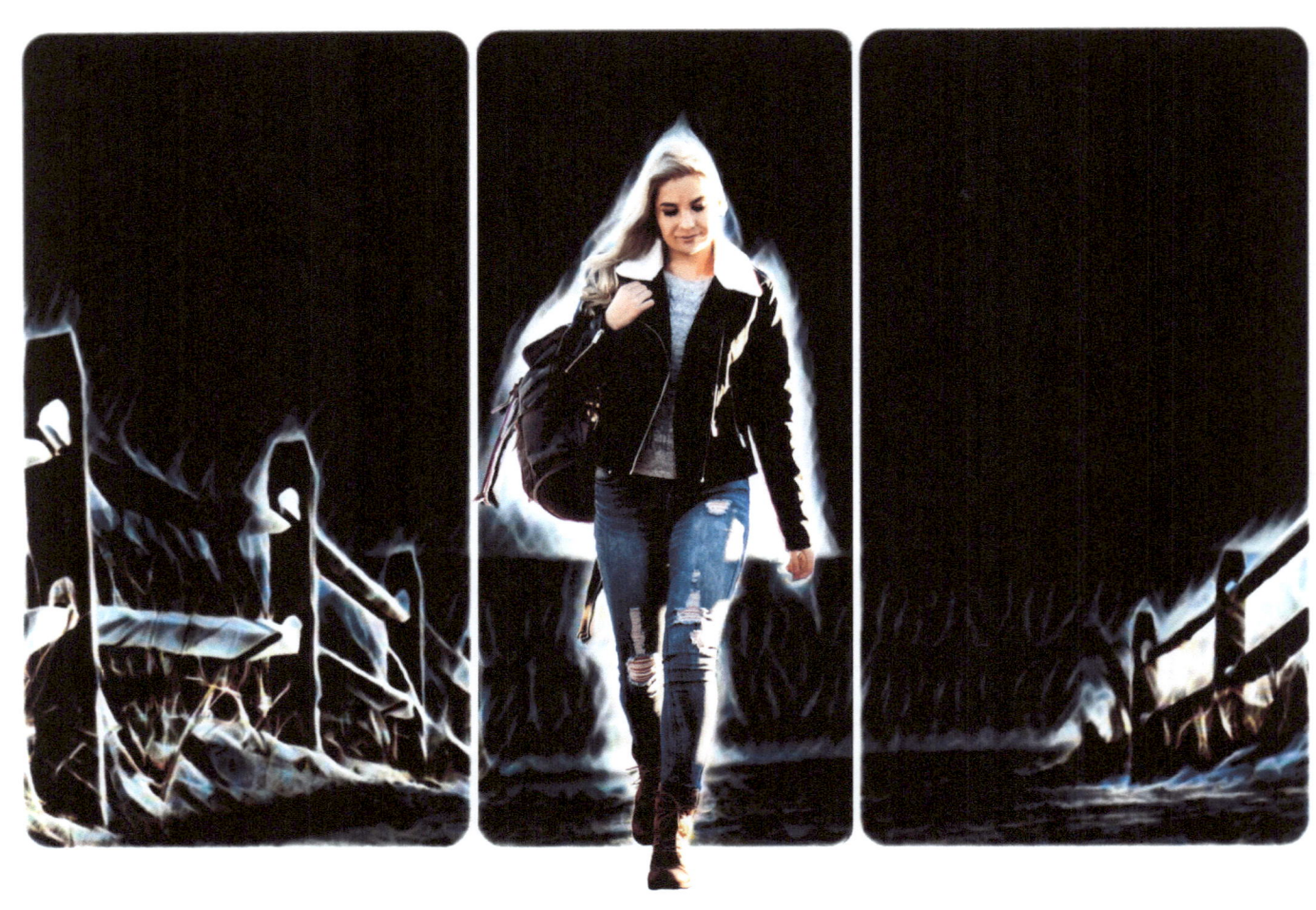

Going away

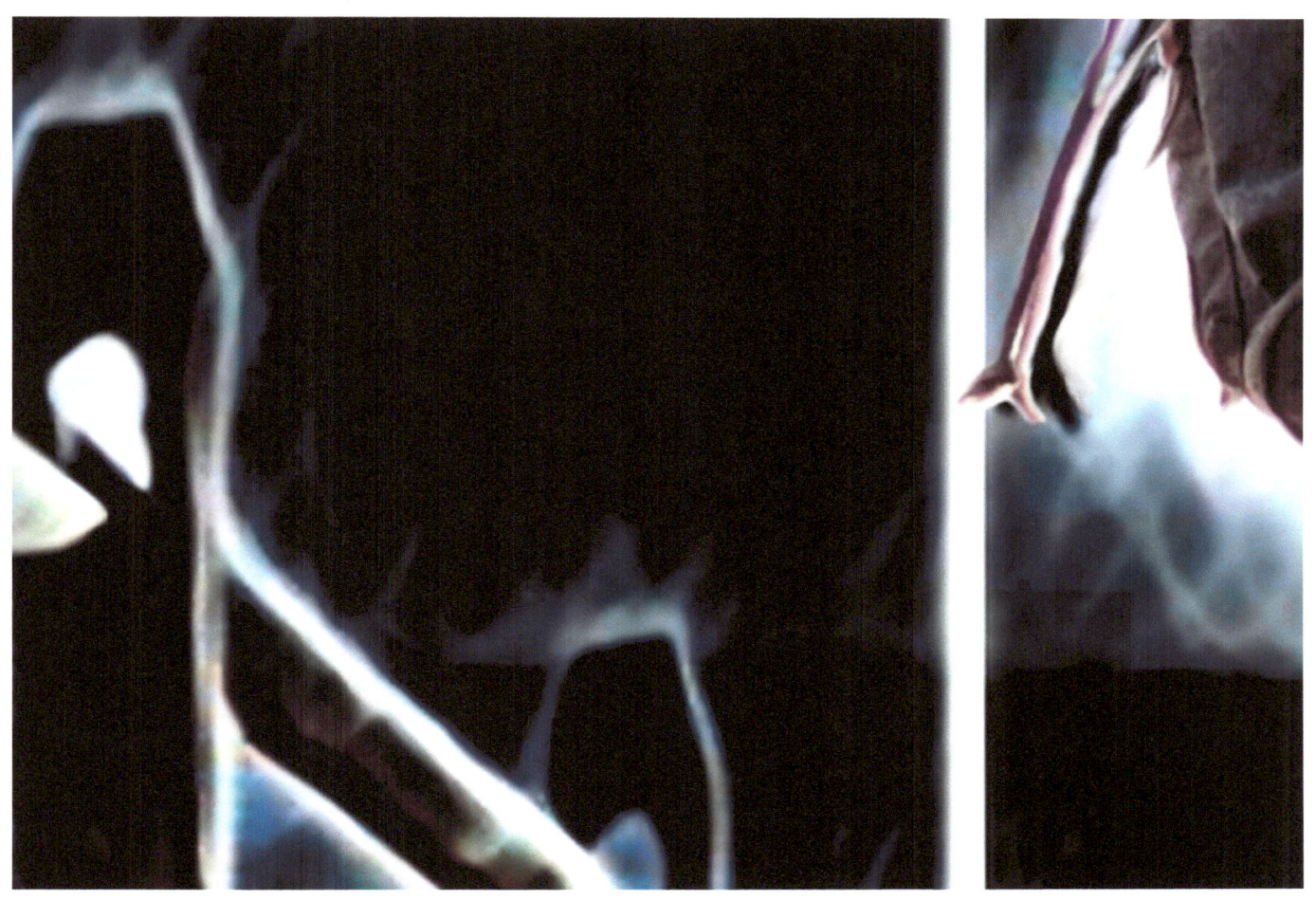

Going away - Detail

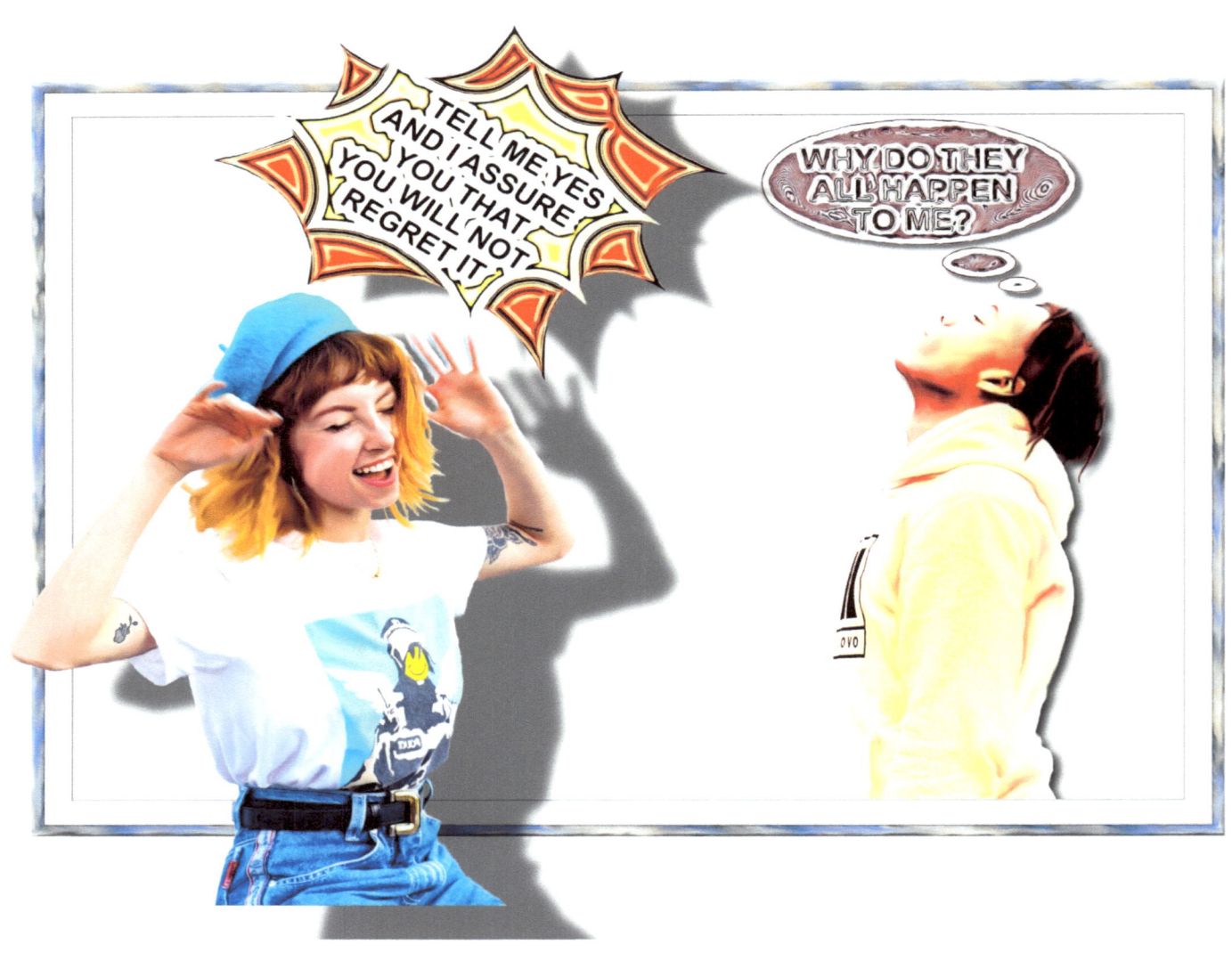

The proposal

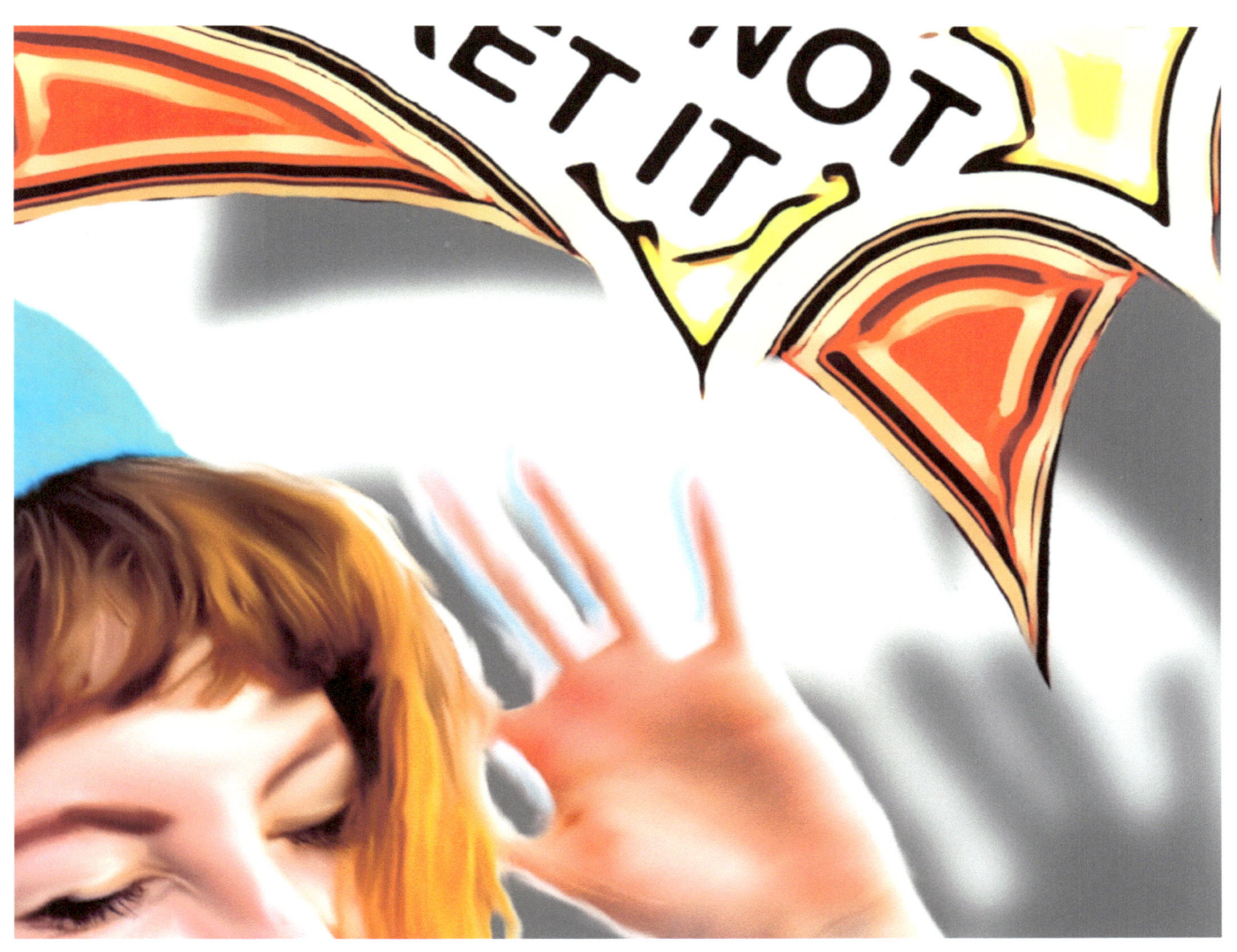

The proposal - Detail

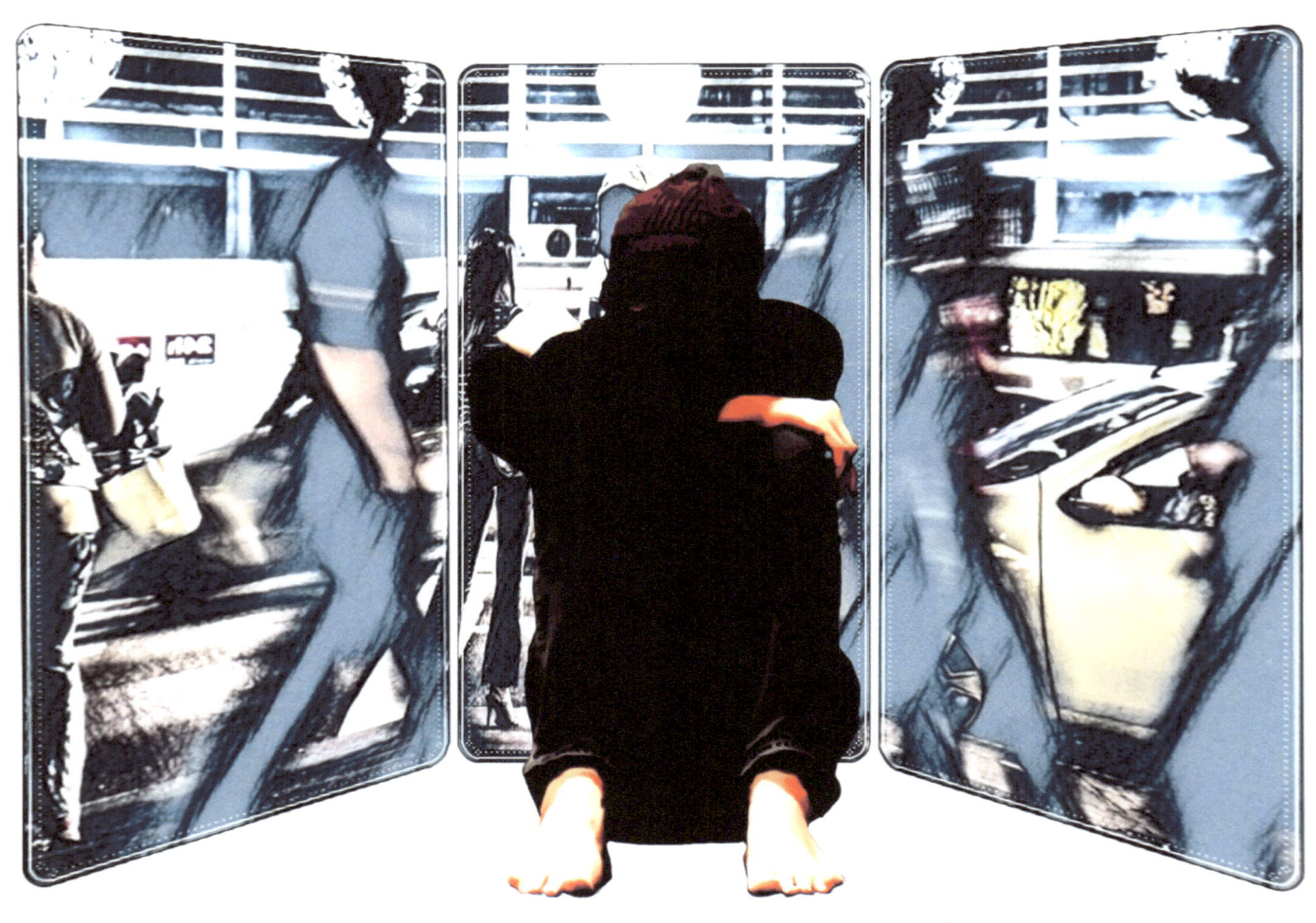

Loneliness

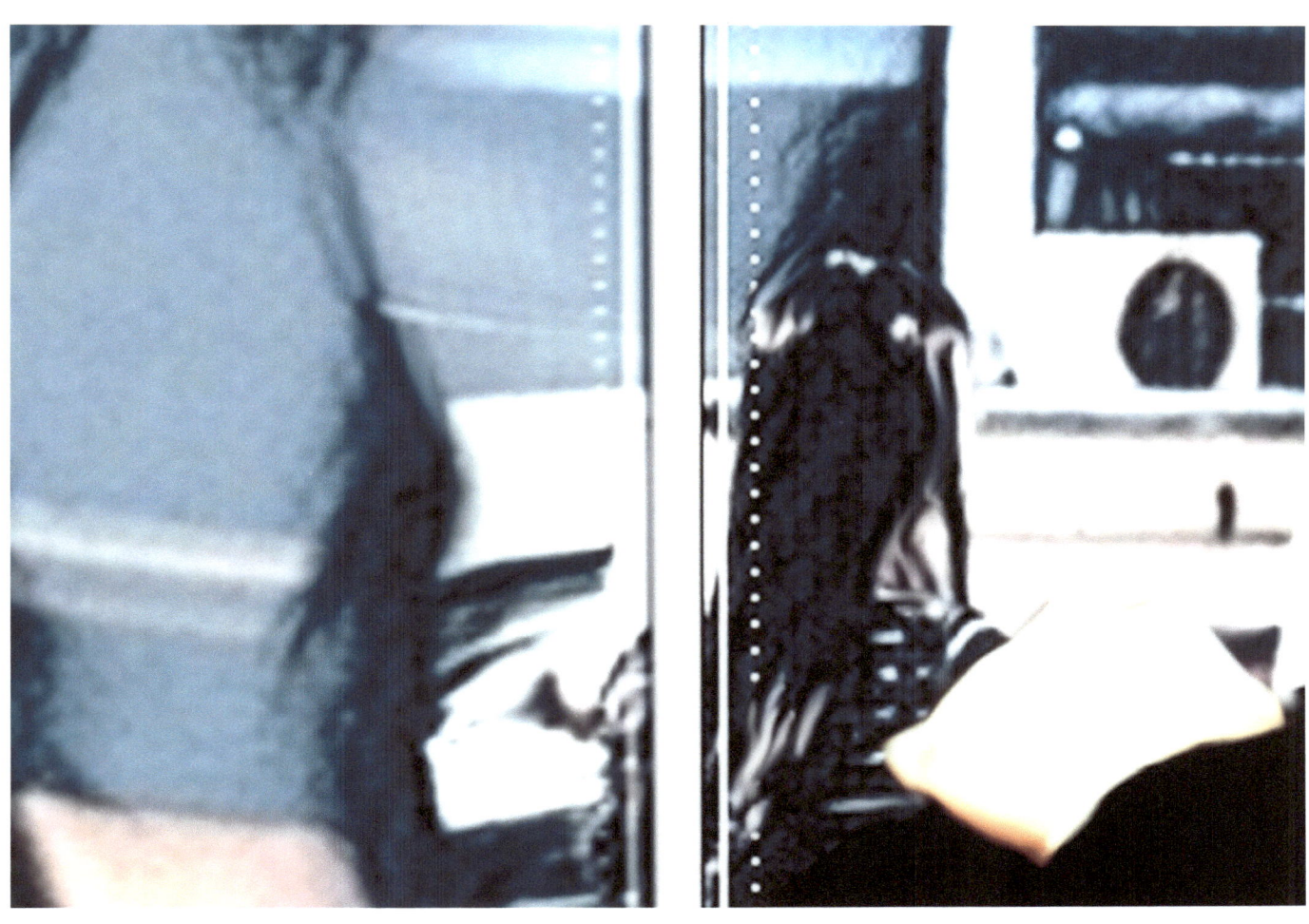

Loneliness - Detail

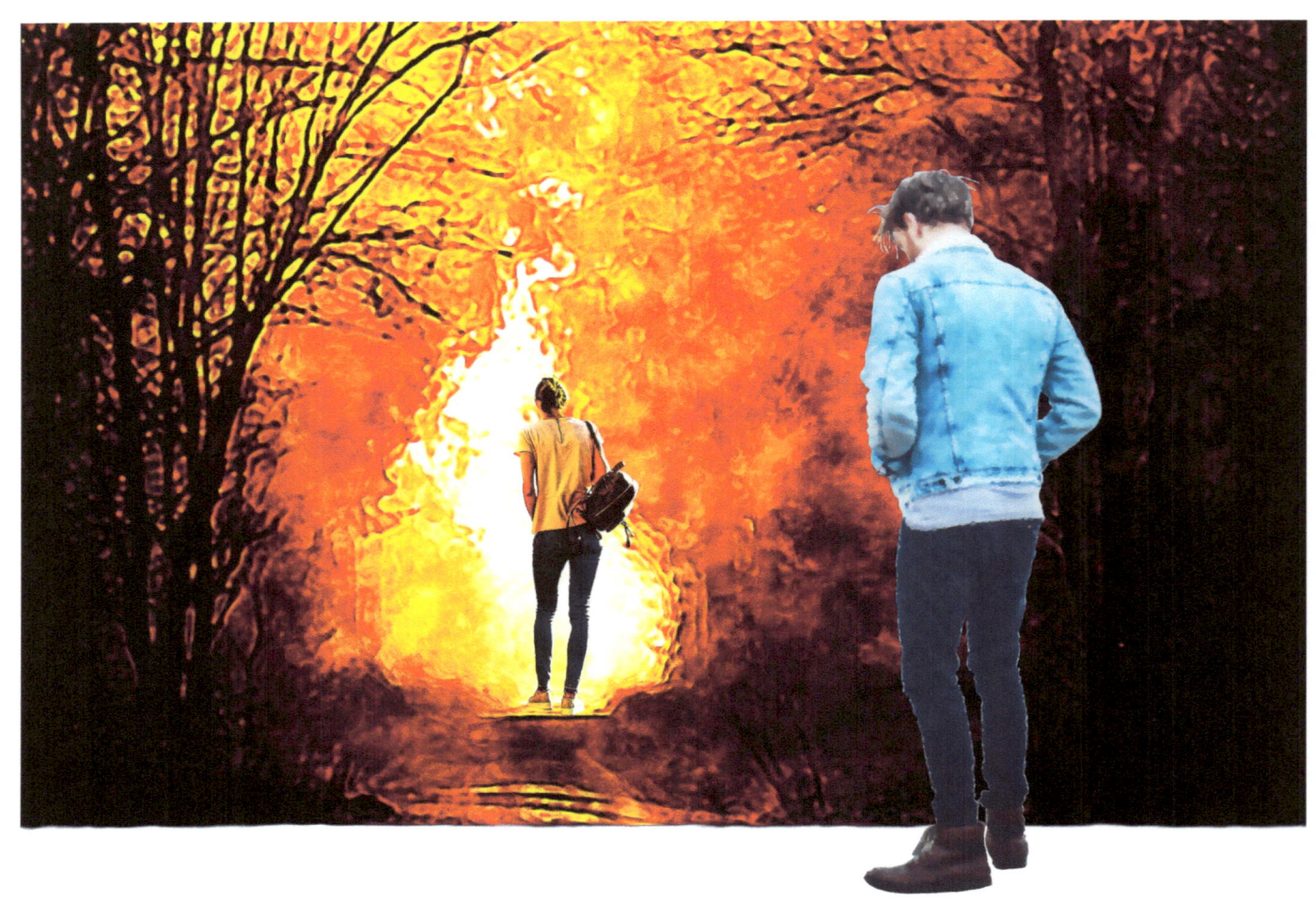

End of a love

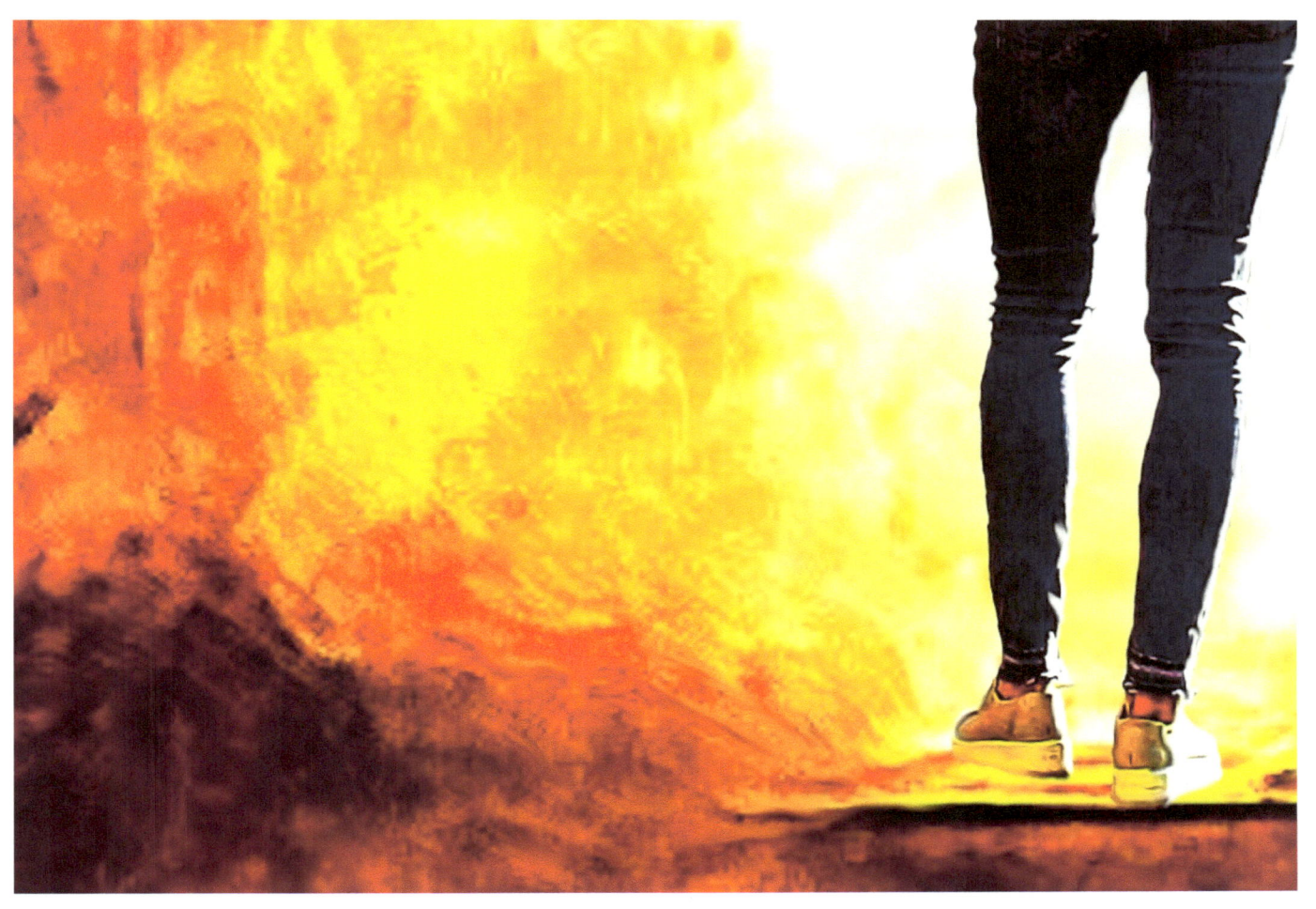

End of a love - Detail

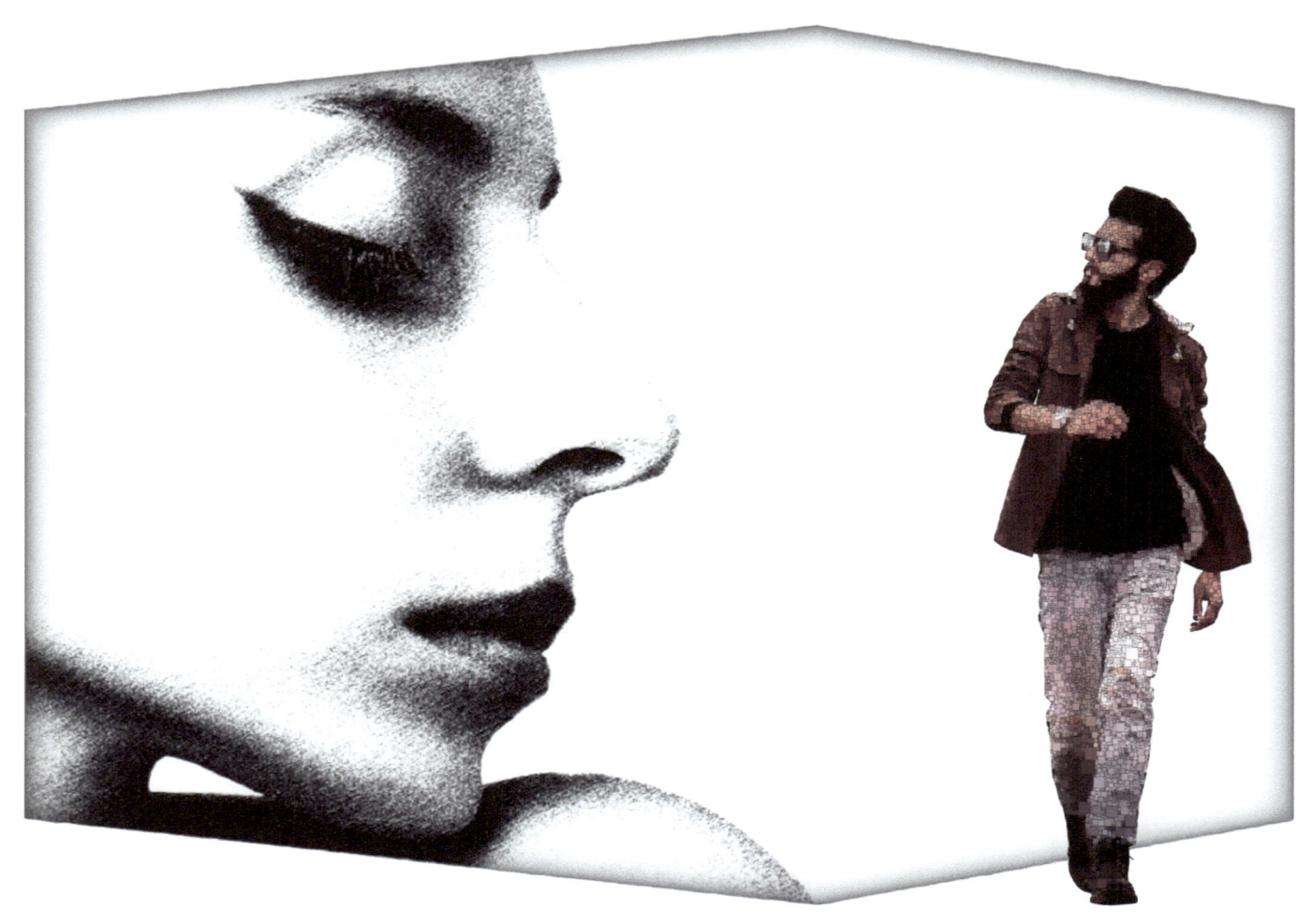

Meeting

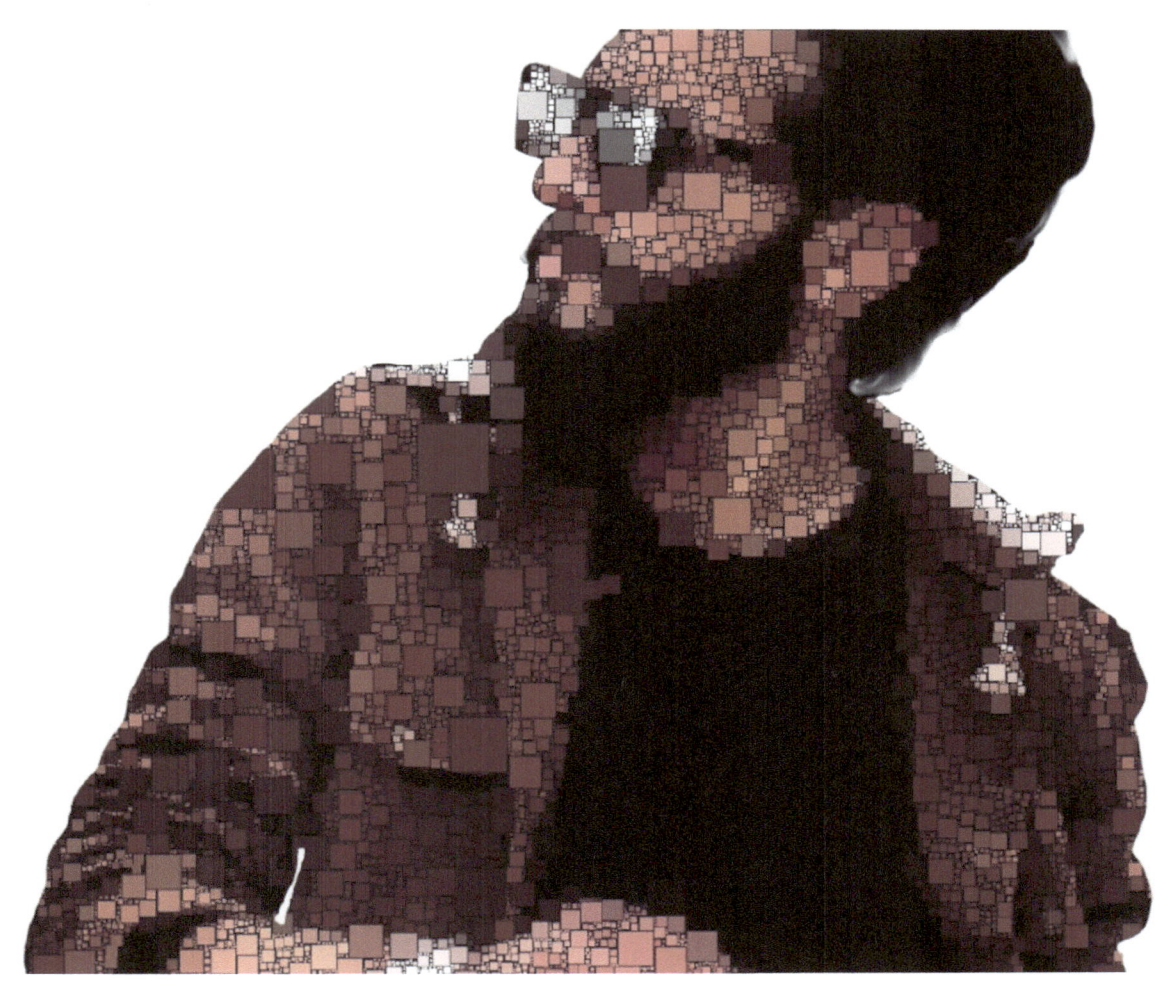

Meeting - Detail

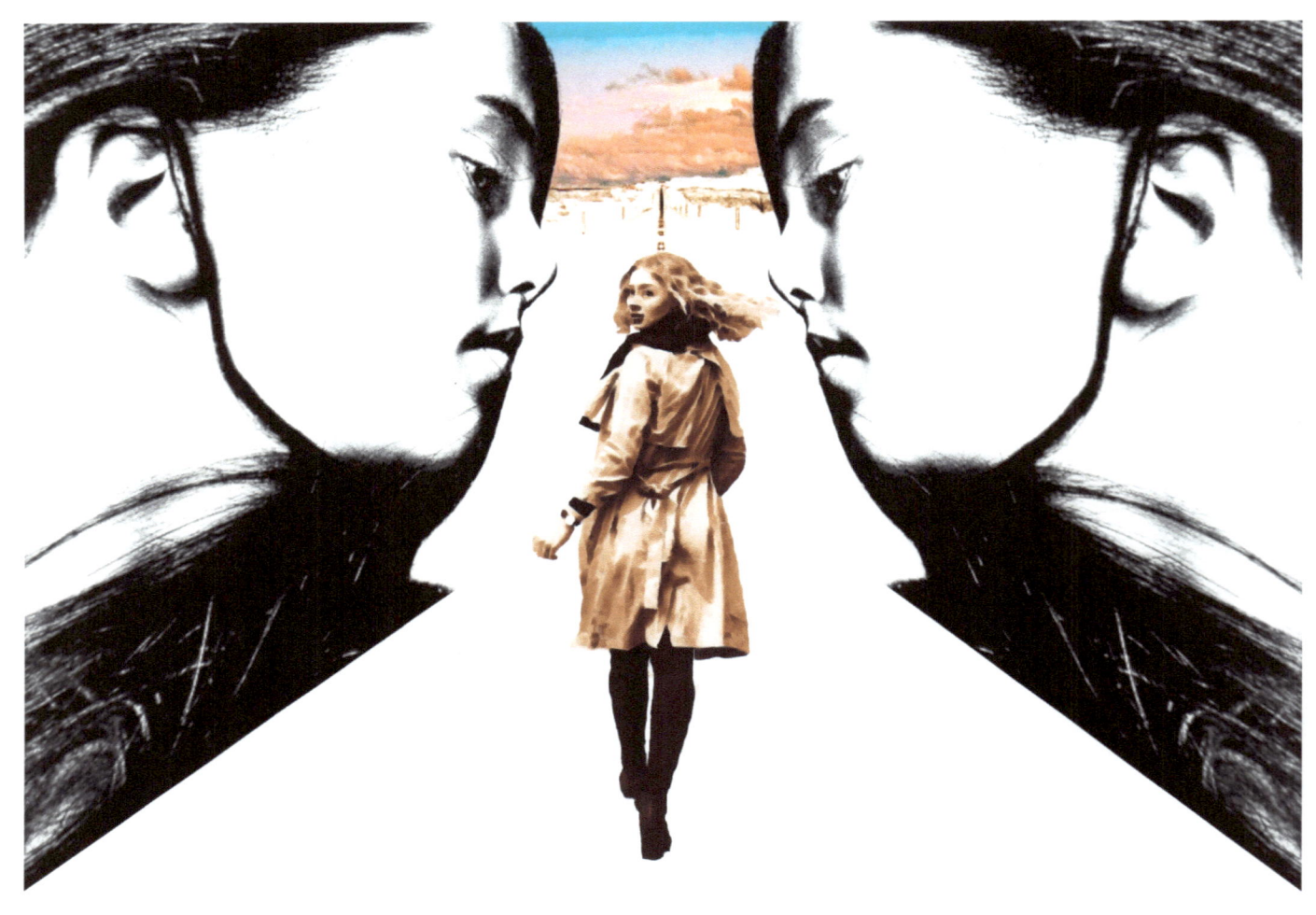

The border

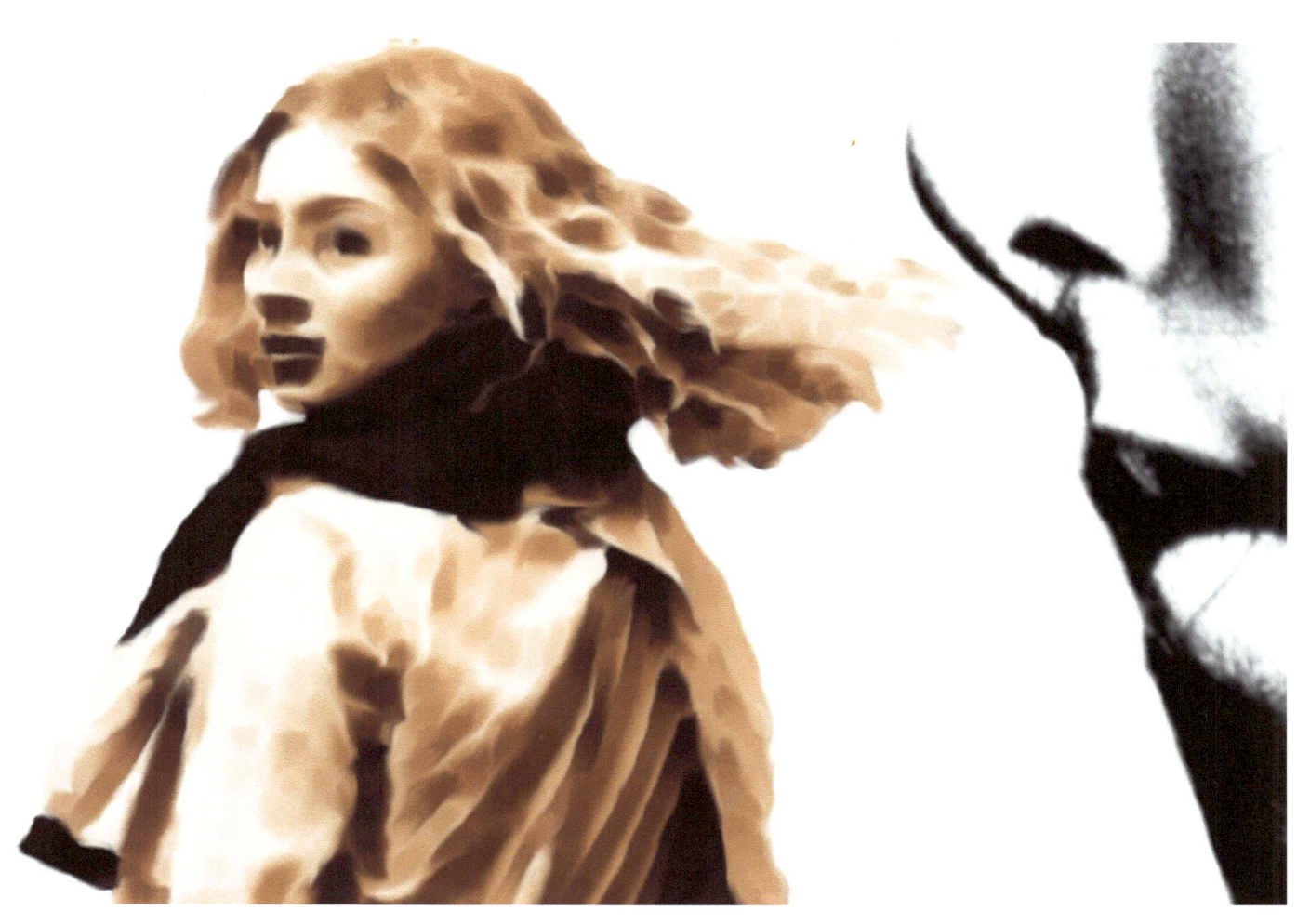

The border - Detail

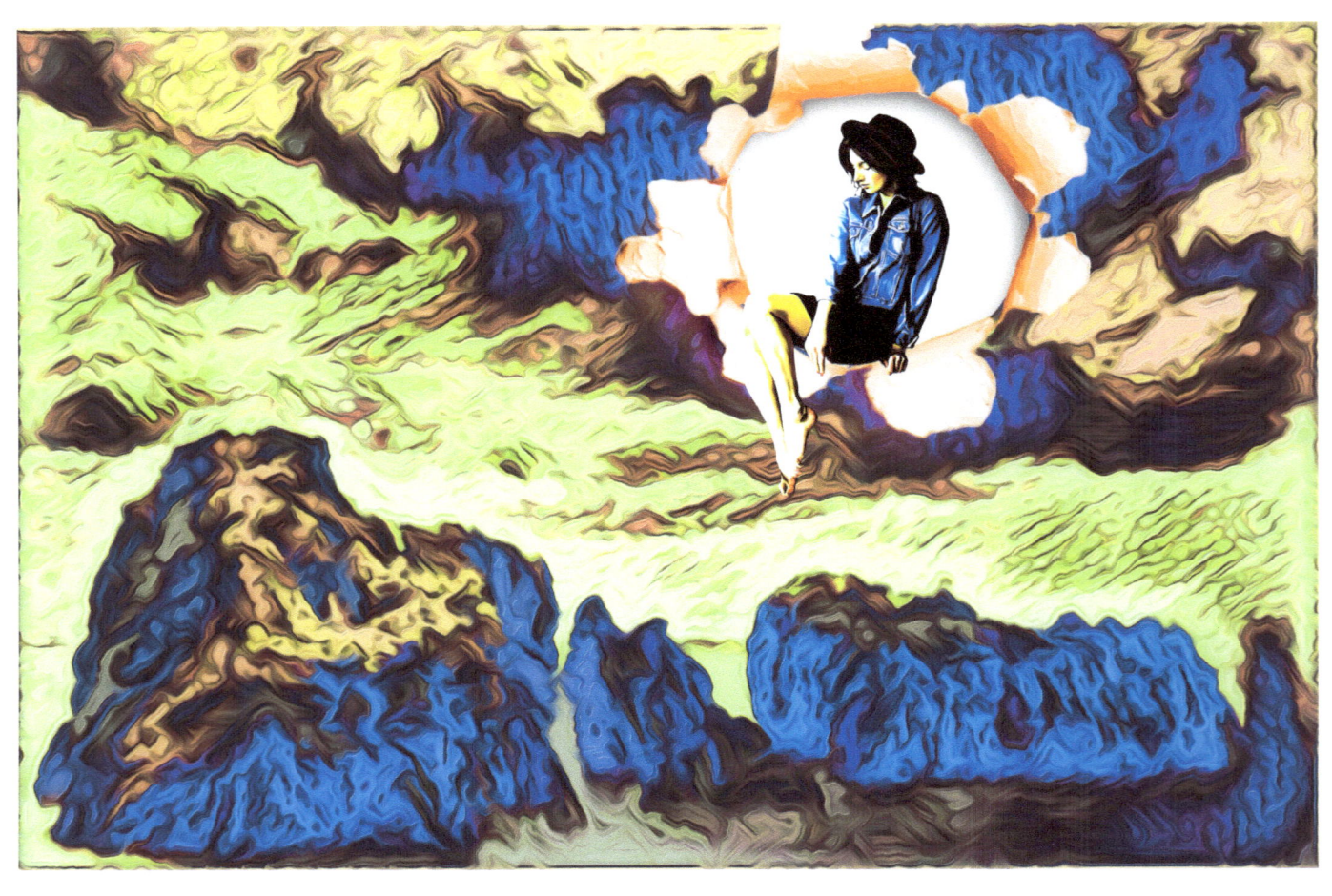

Window with blue view

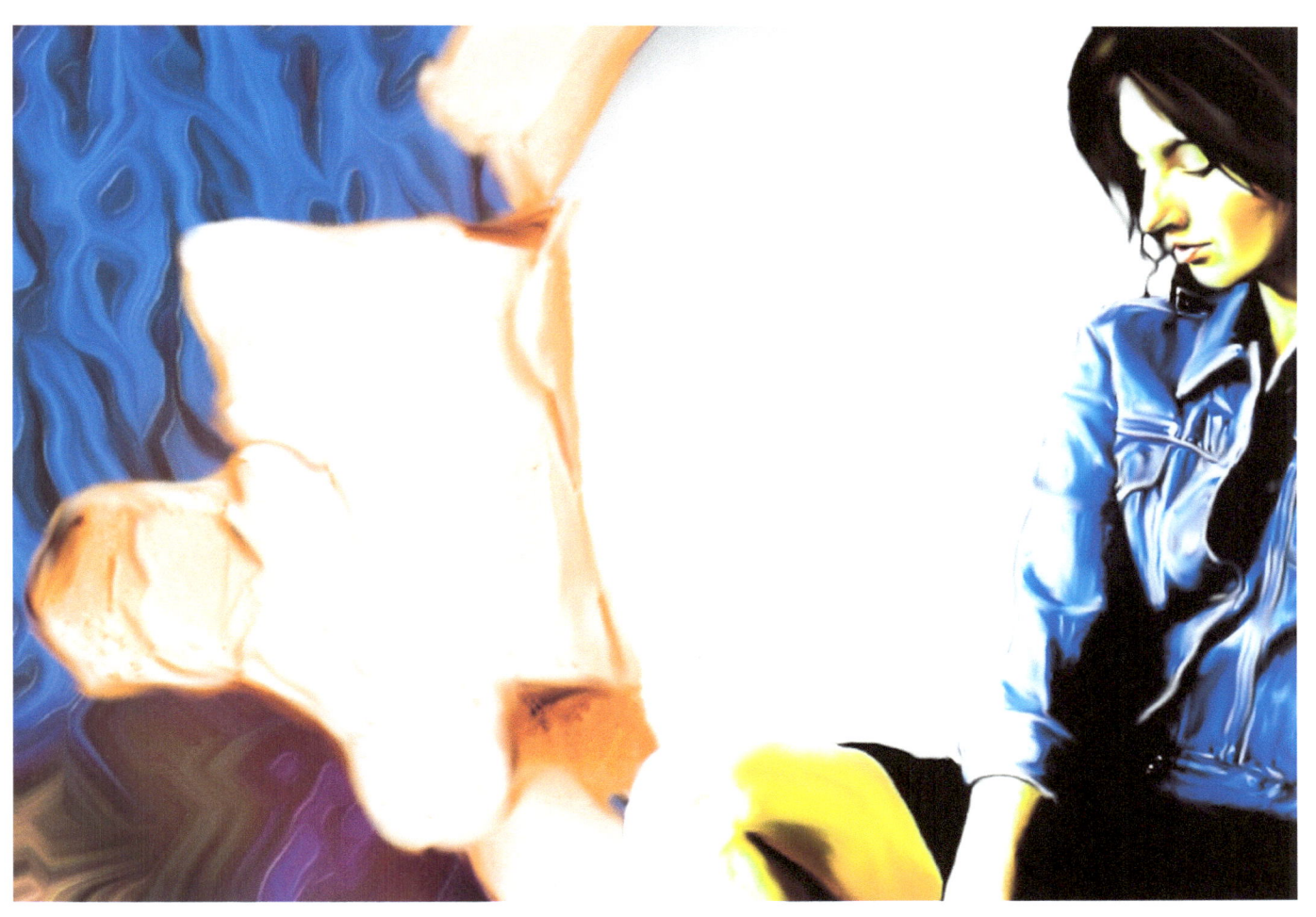

Window with blue view - Detail

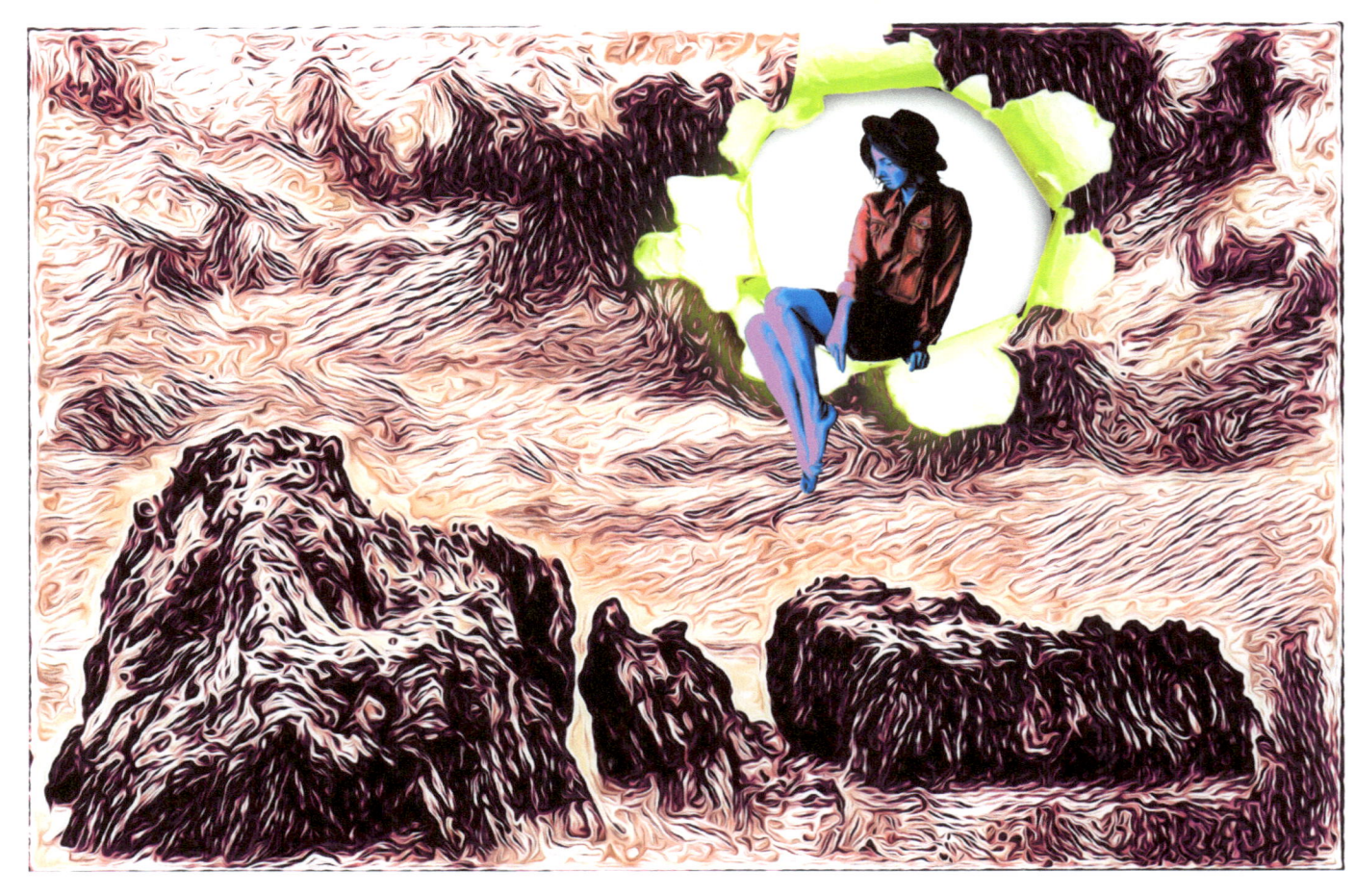

Window with purple view

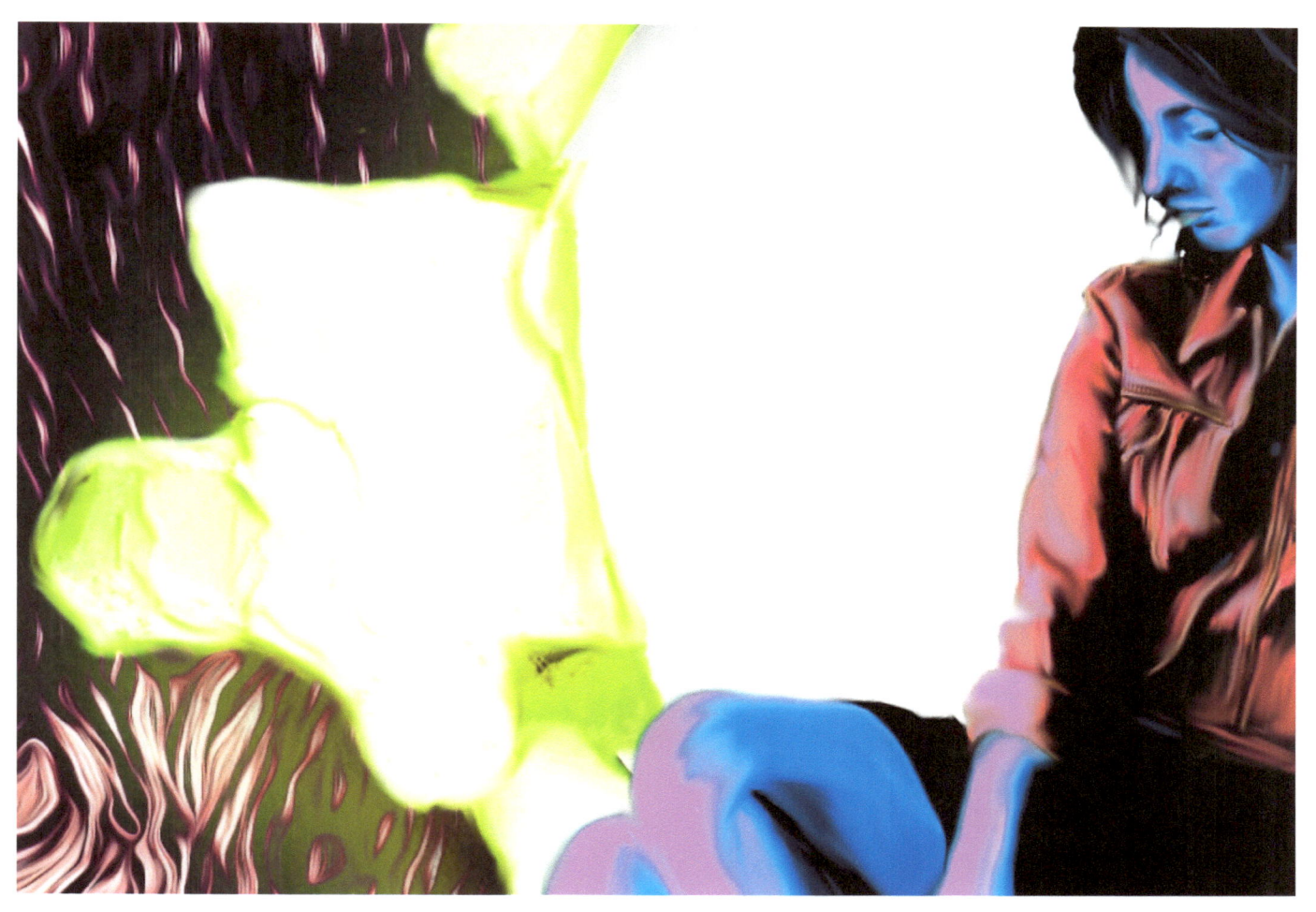

Window with purple view - Detail

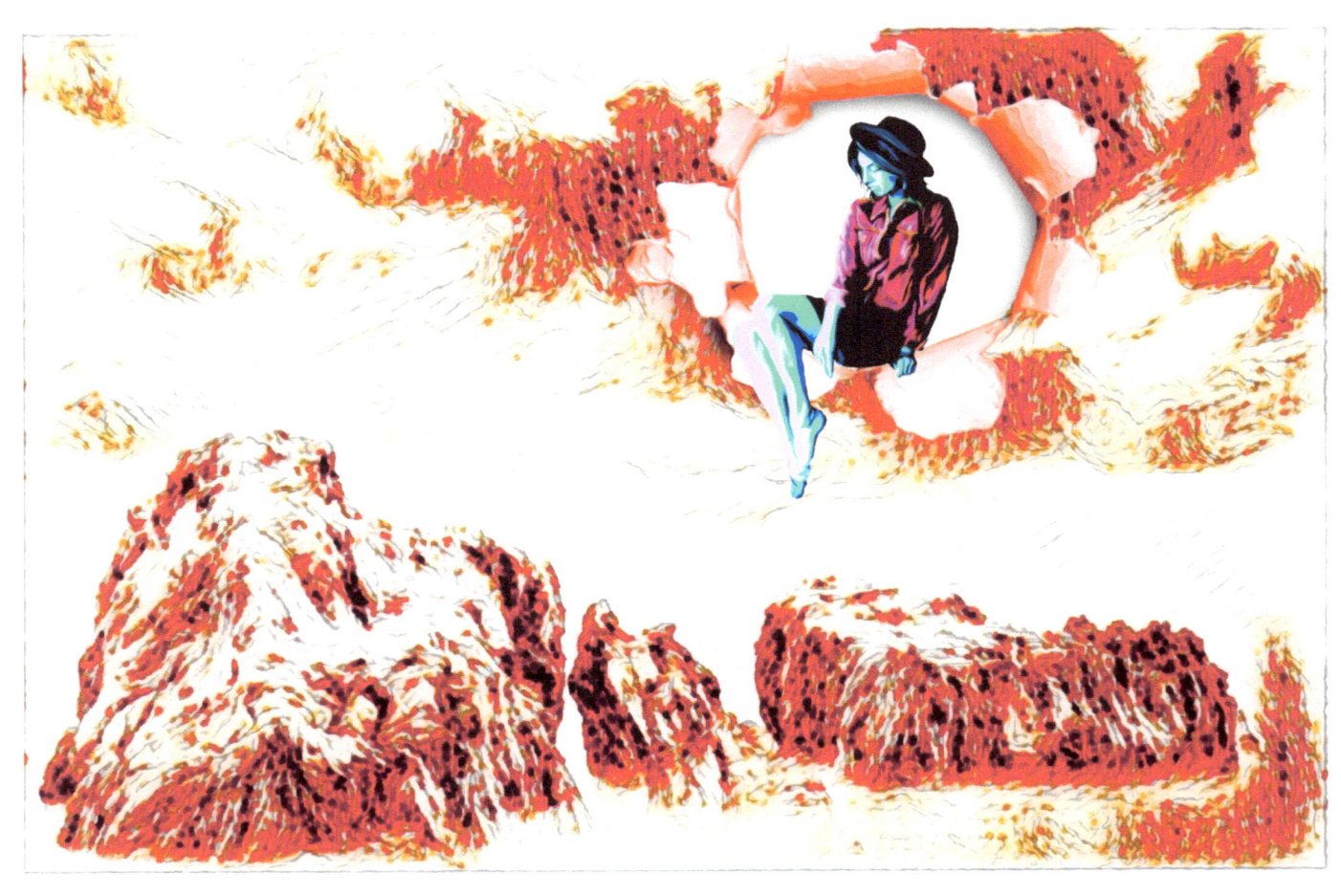

Window with red view

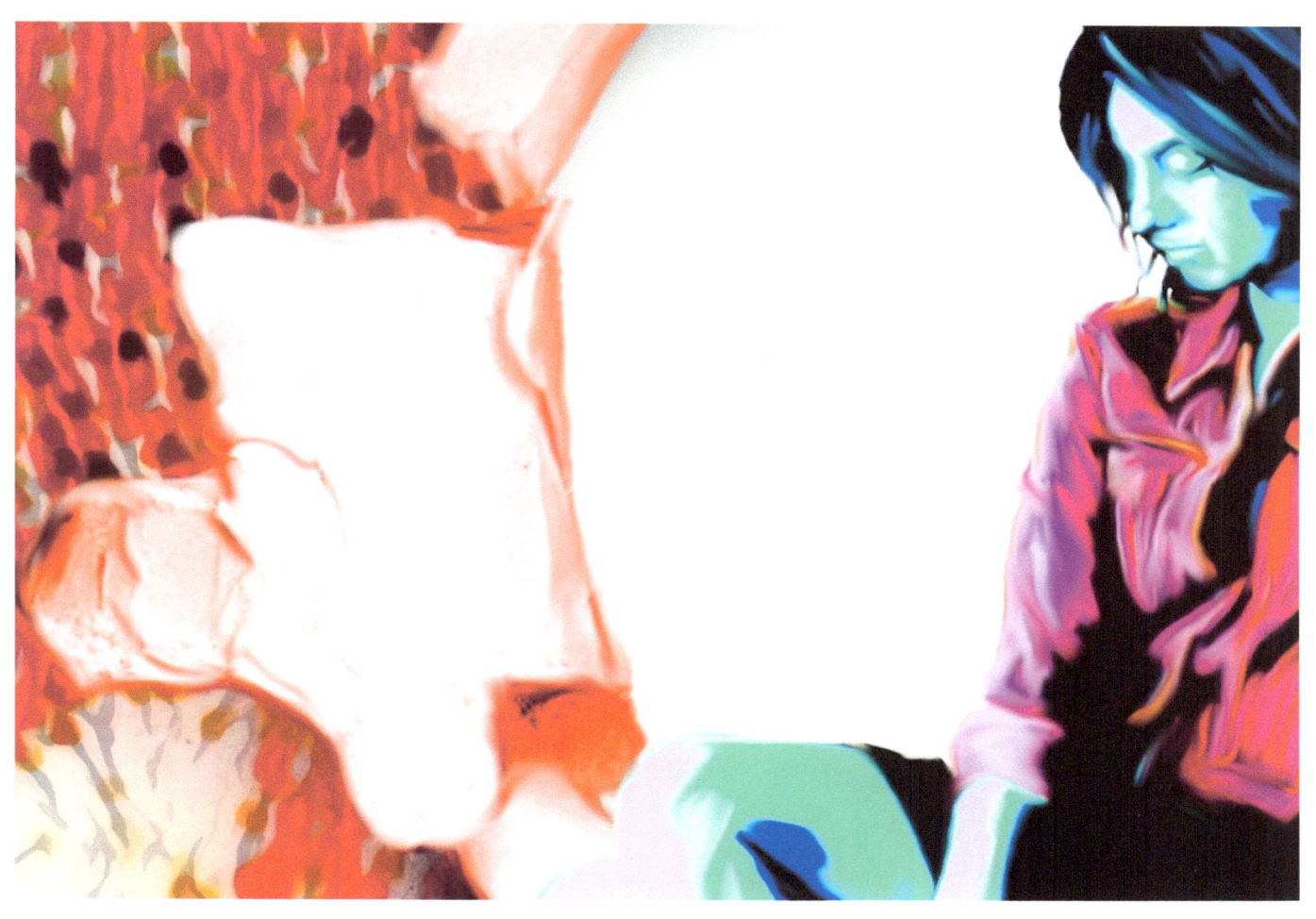

Window with red view - Detail

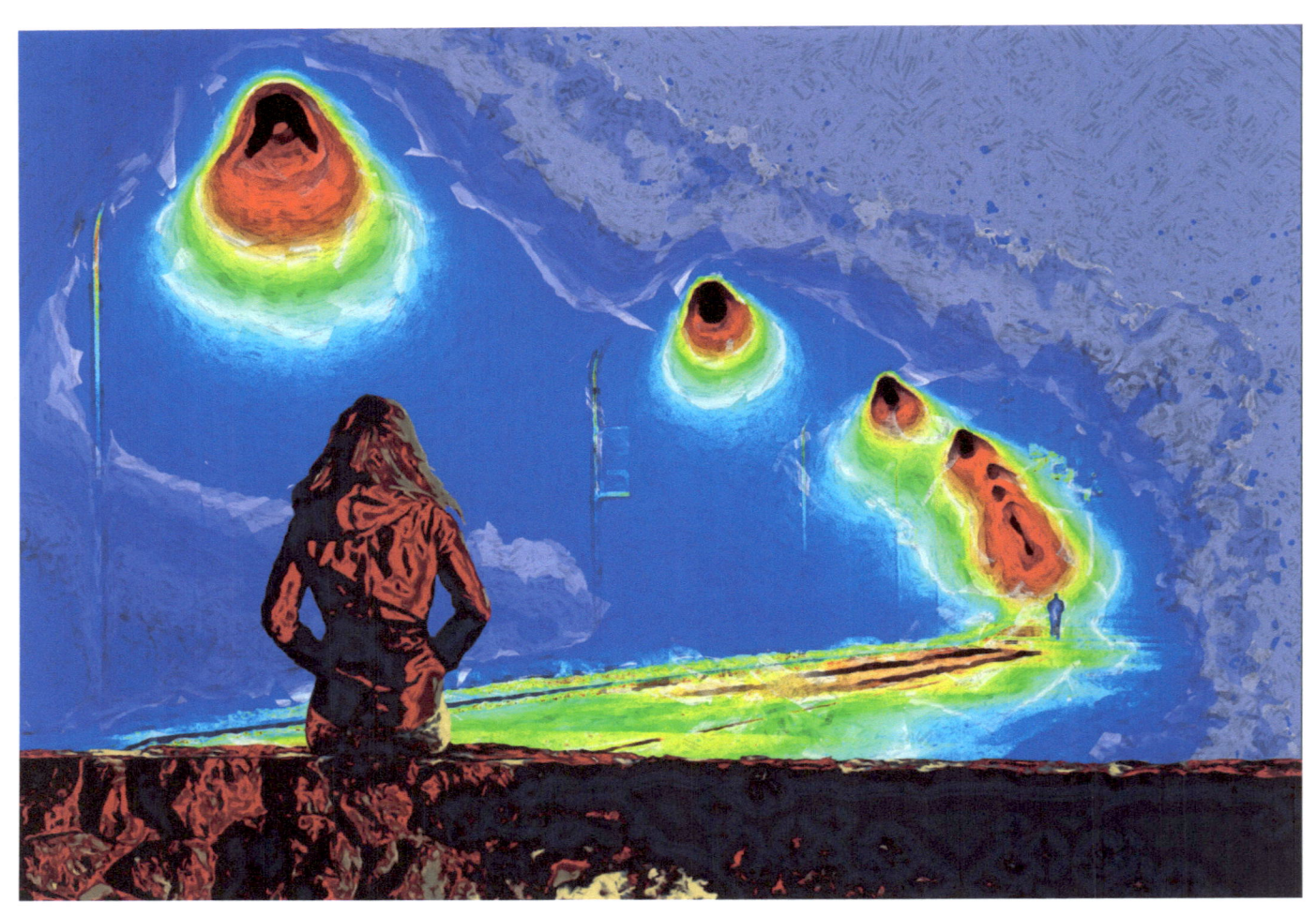

The road

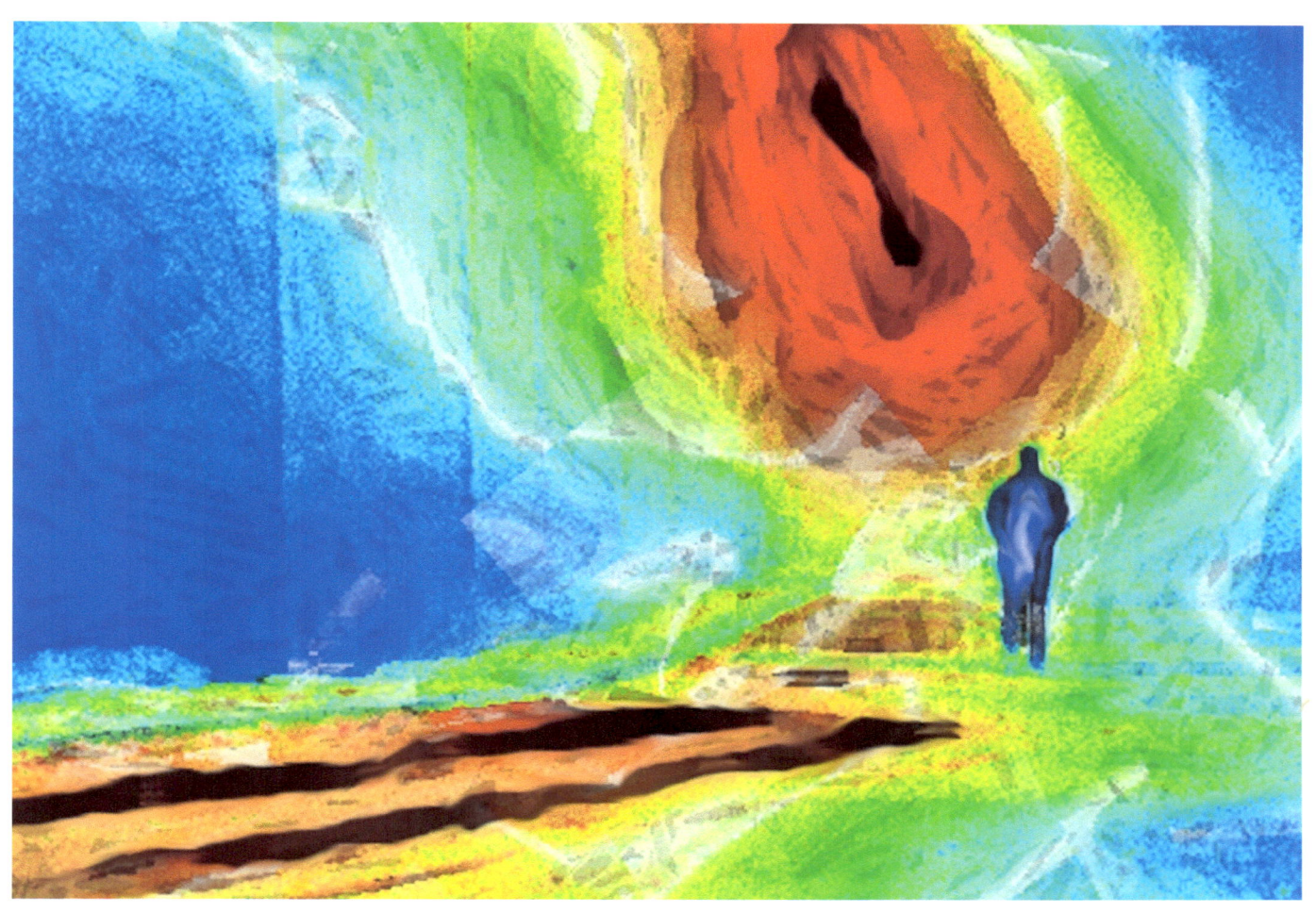

The road - Detail

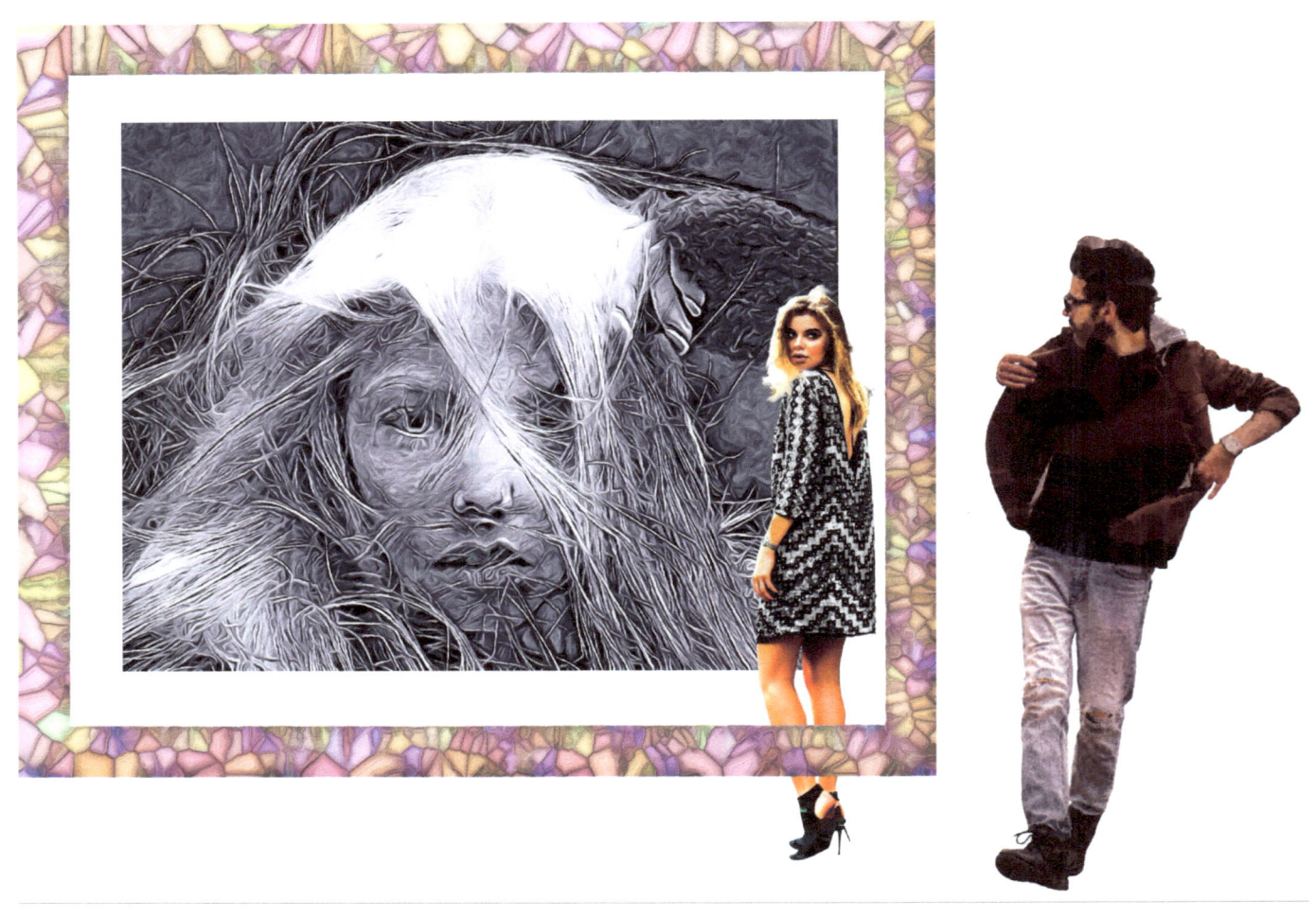

Farewell

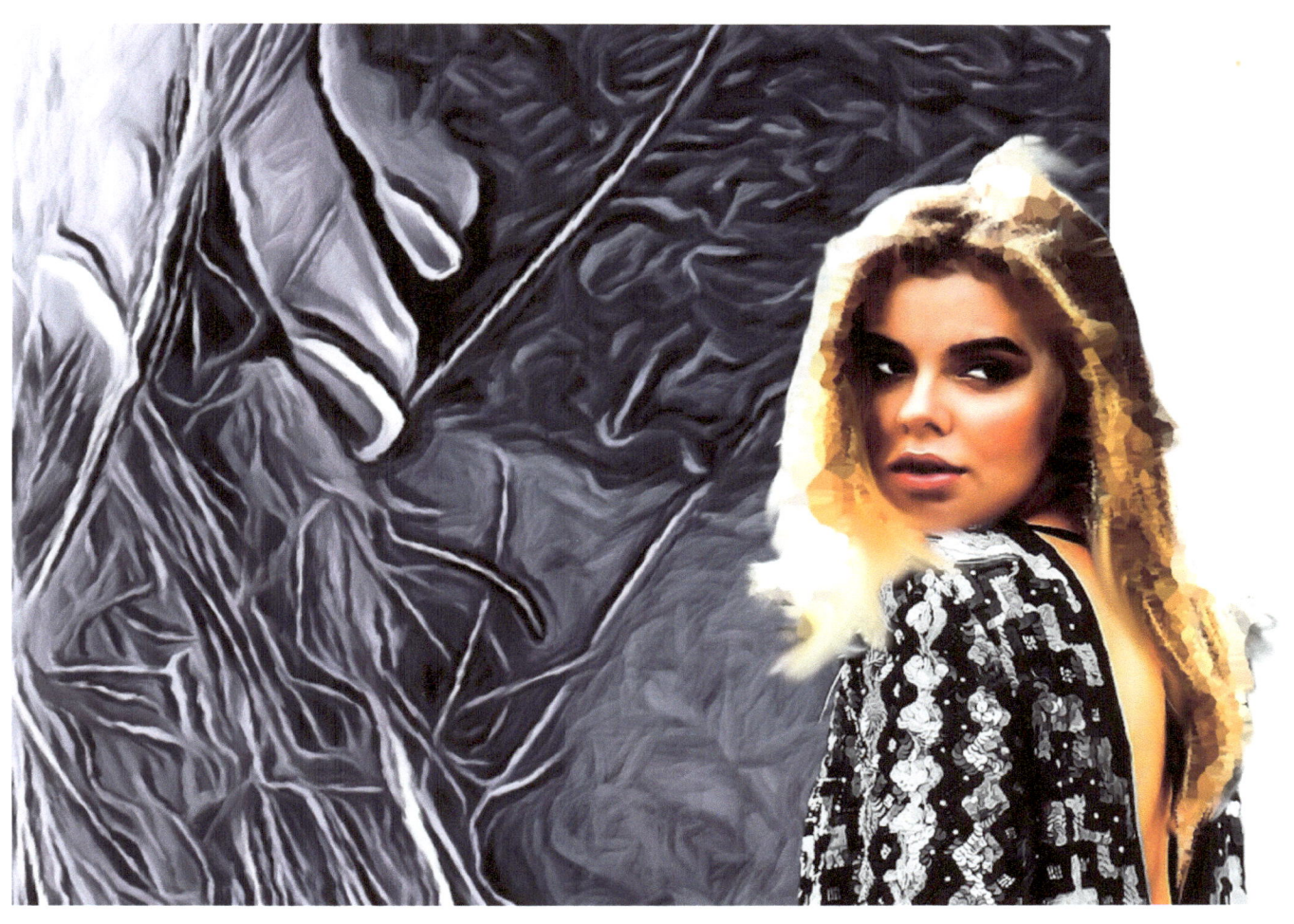

Farewell - Detail

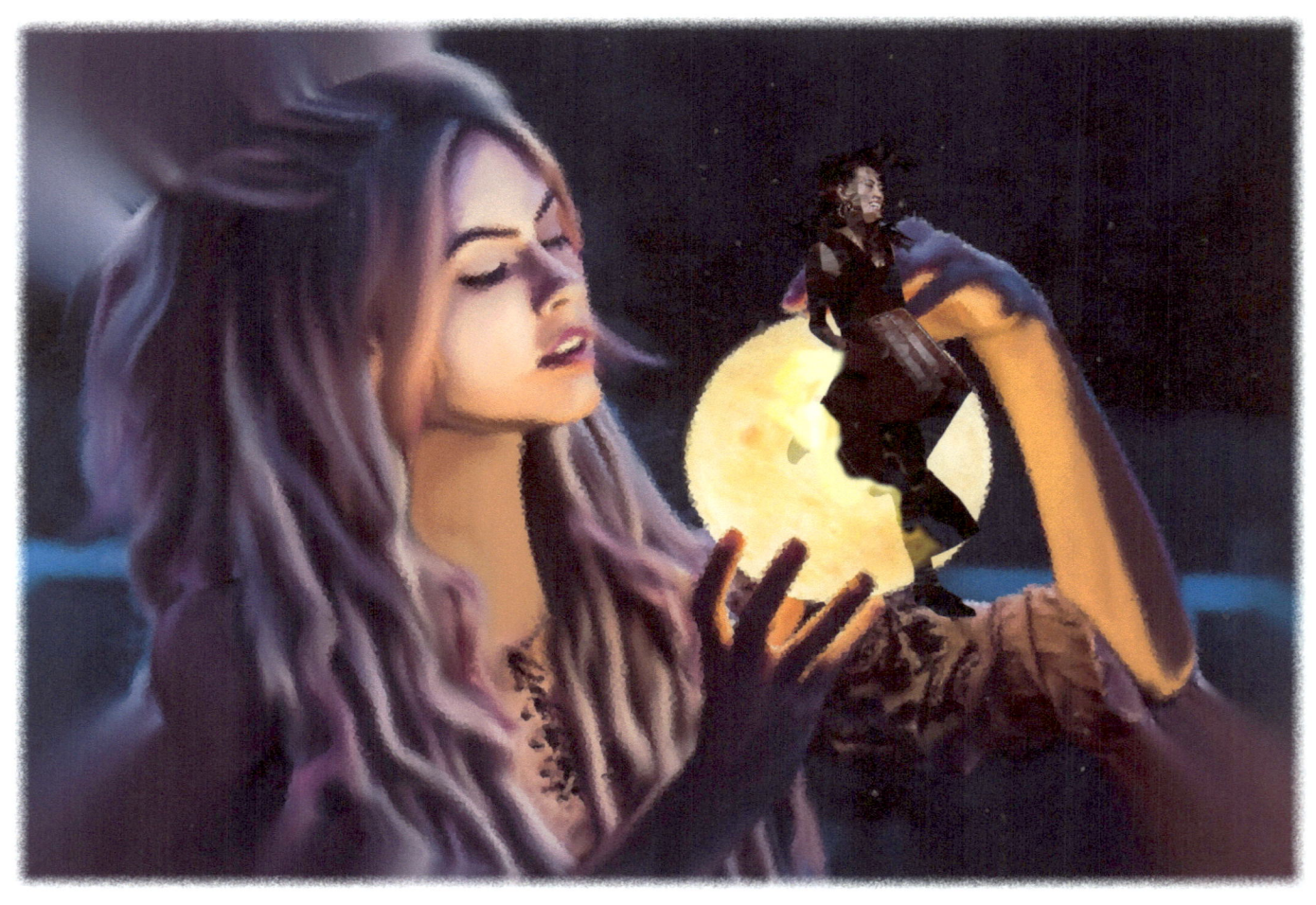

Going away

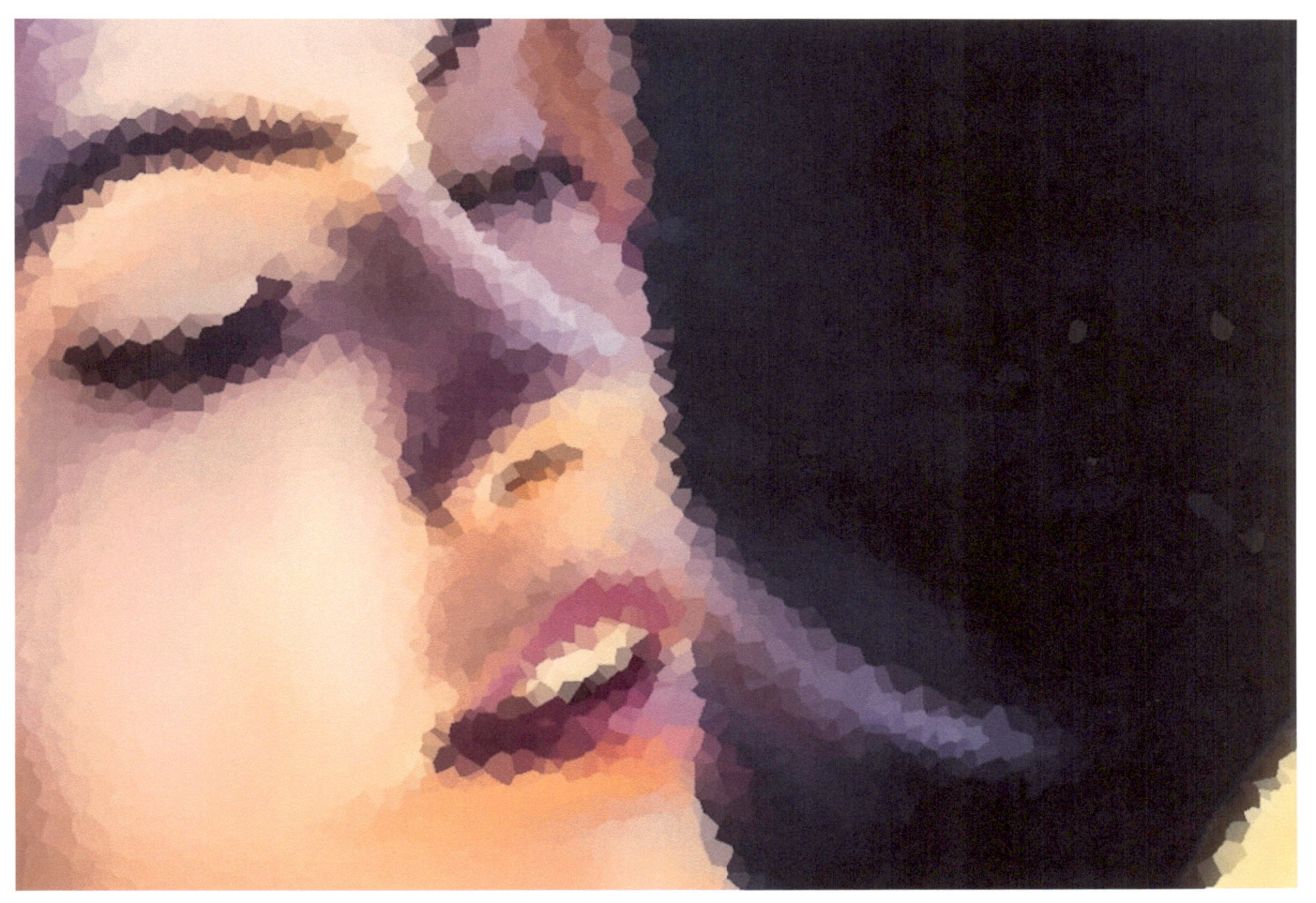

Going away - Detail

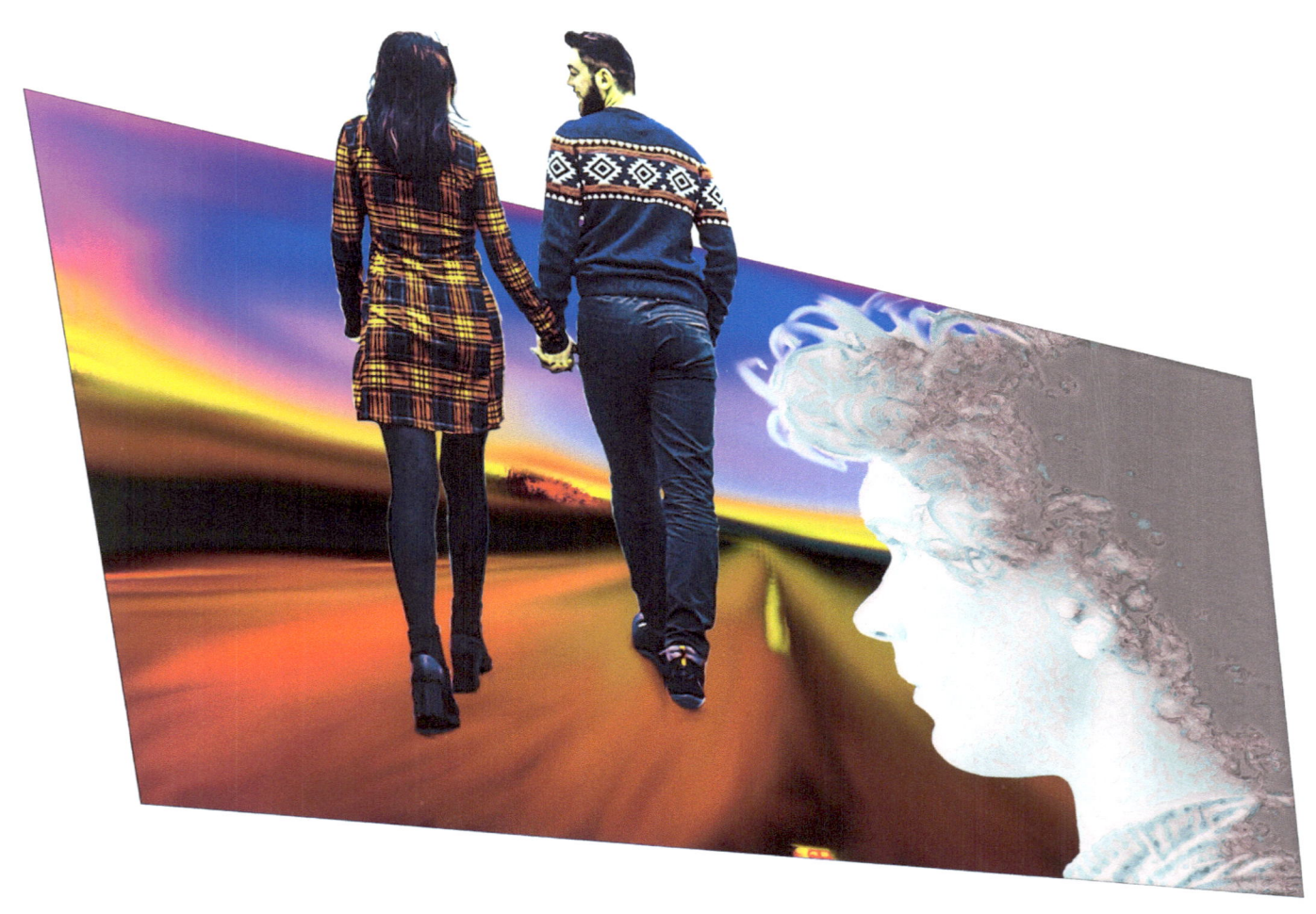

Past, present and future

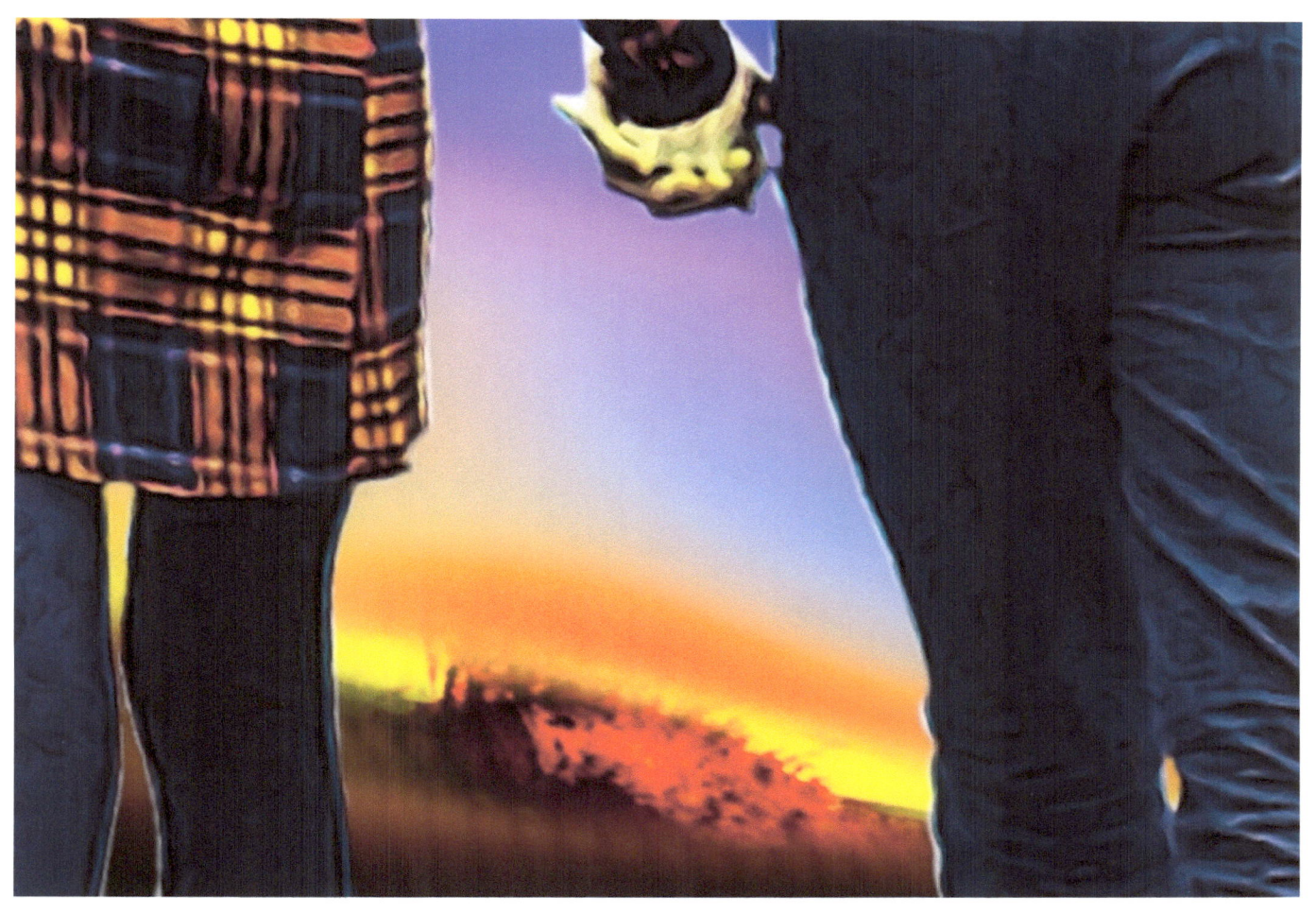

Past, present and future - Detail

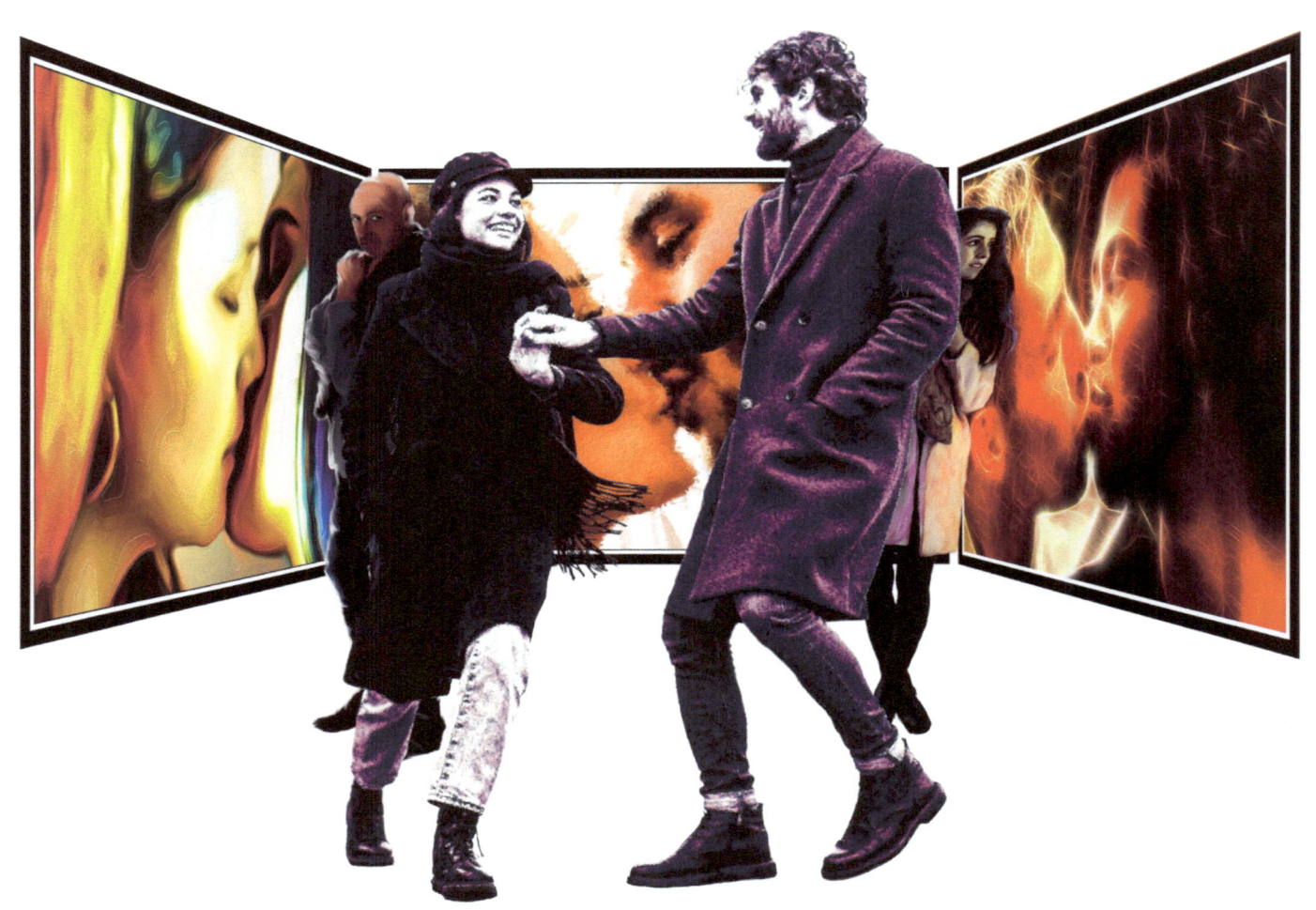

The kiss

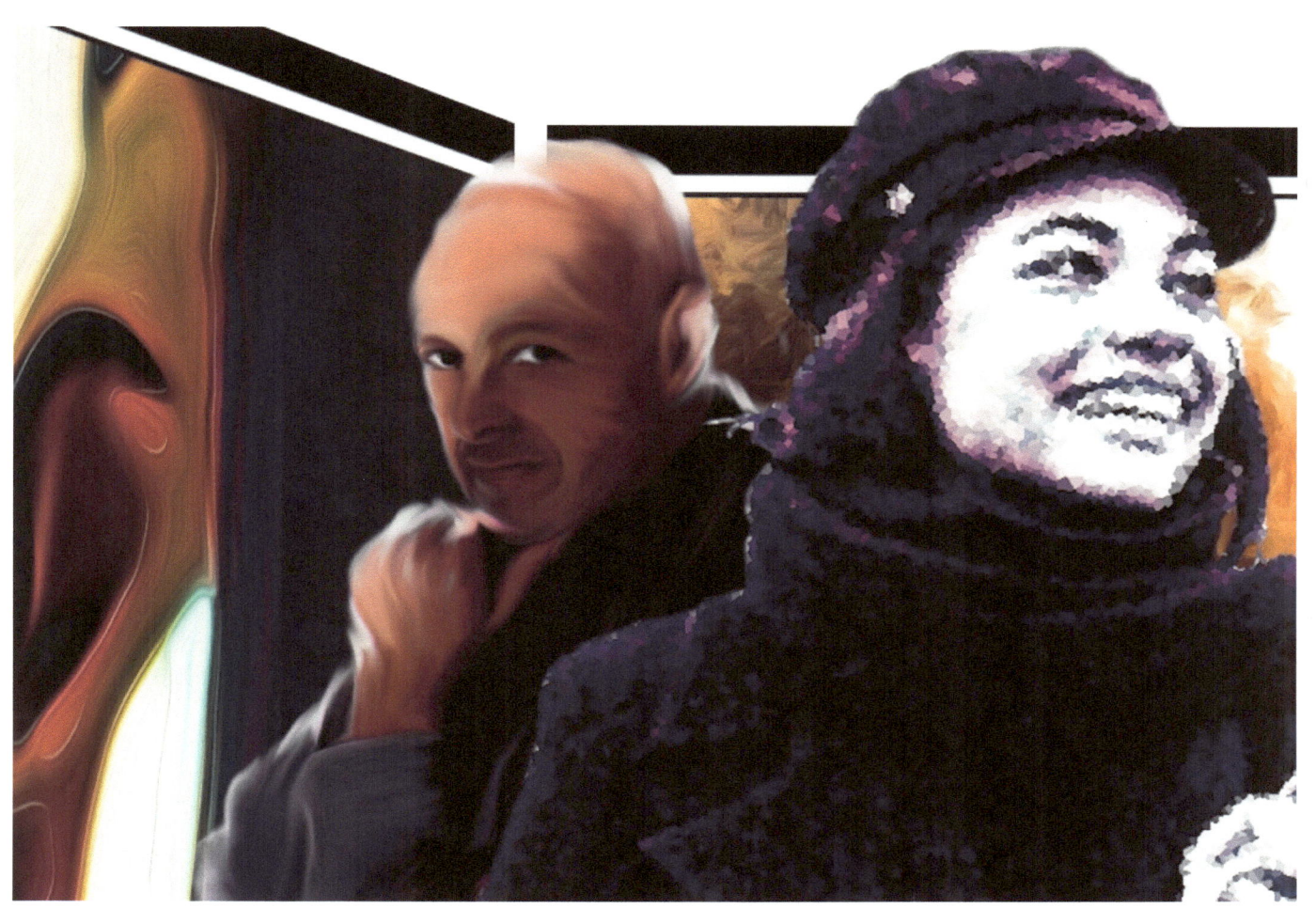

The kiss - Detail one

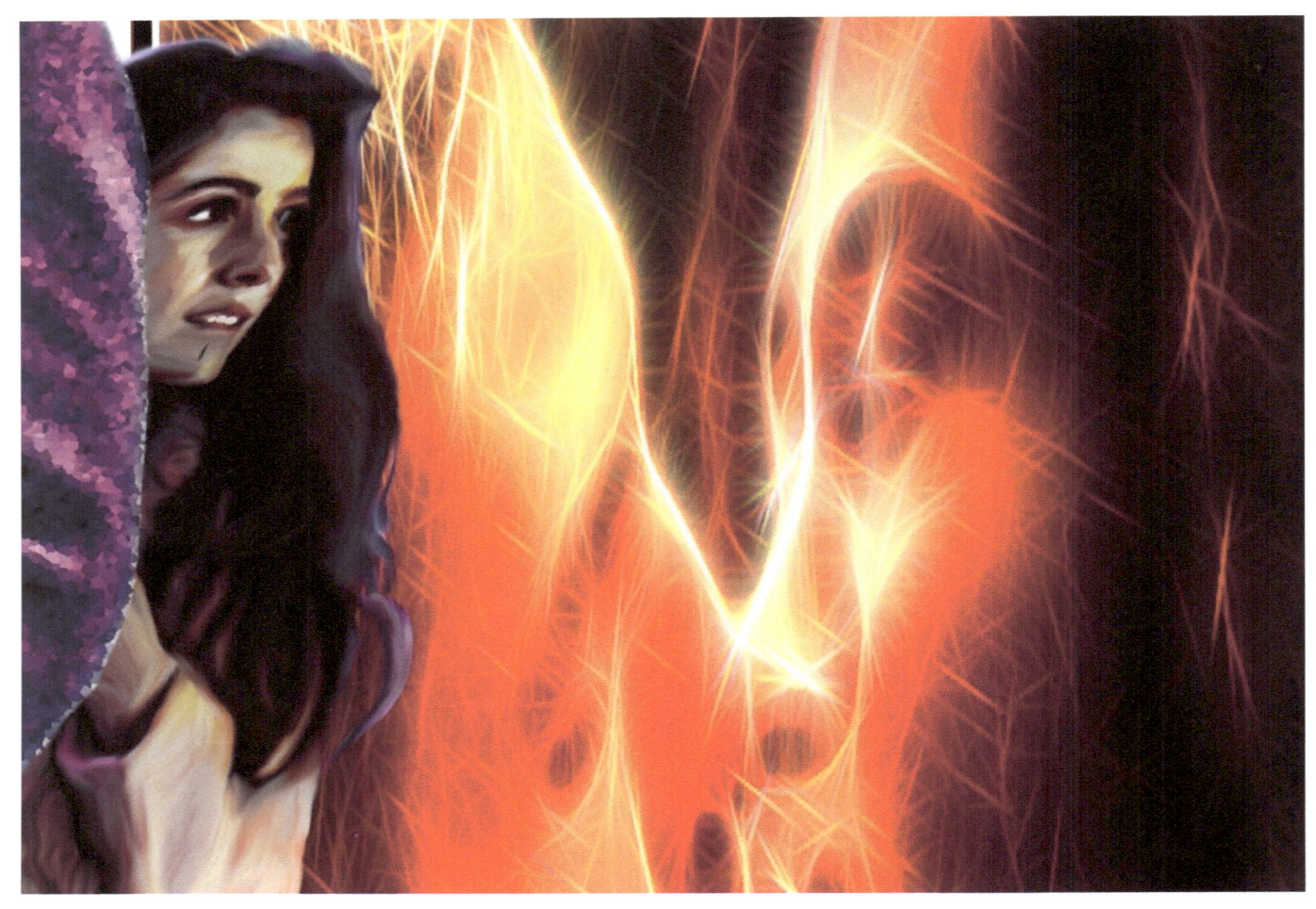

The kiss - Detail two

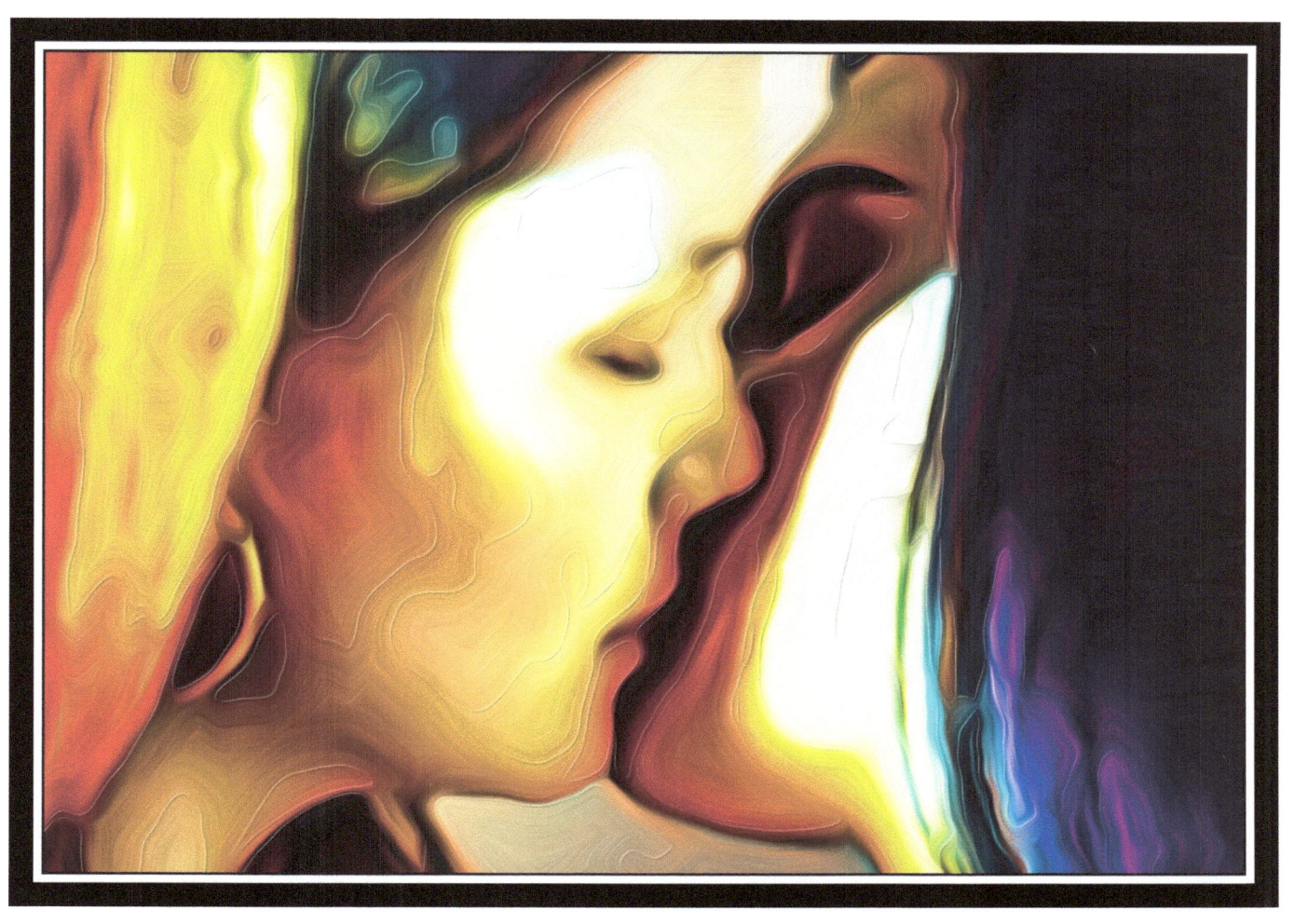

The kiss - Picture on the left

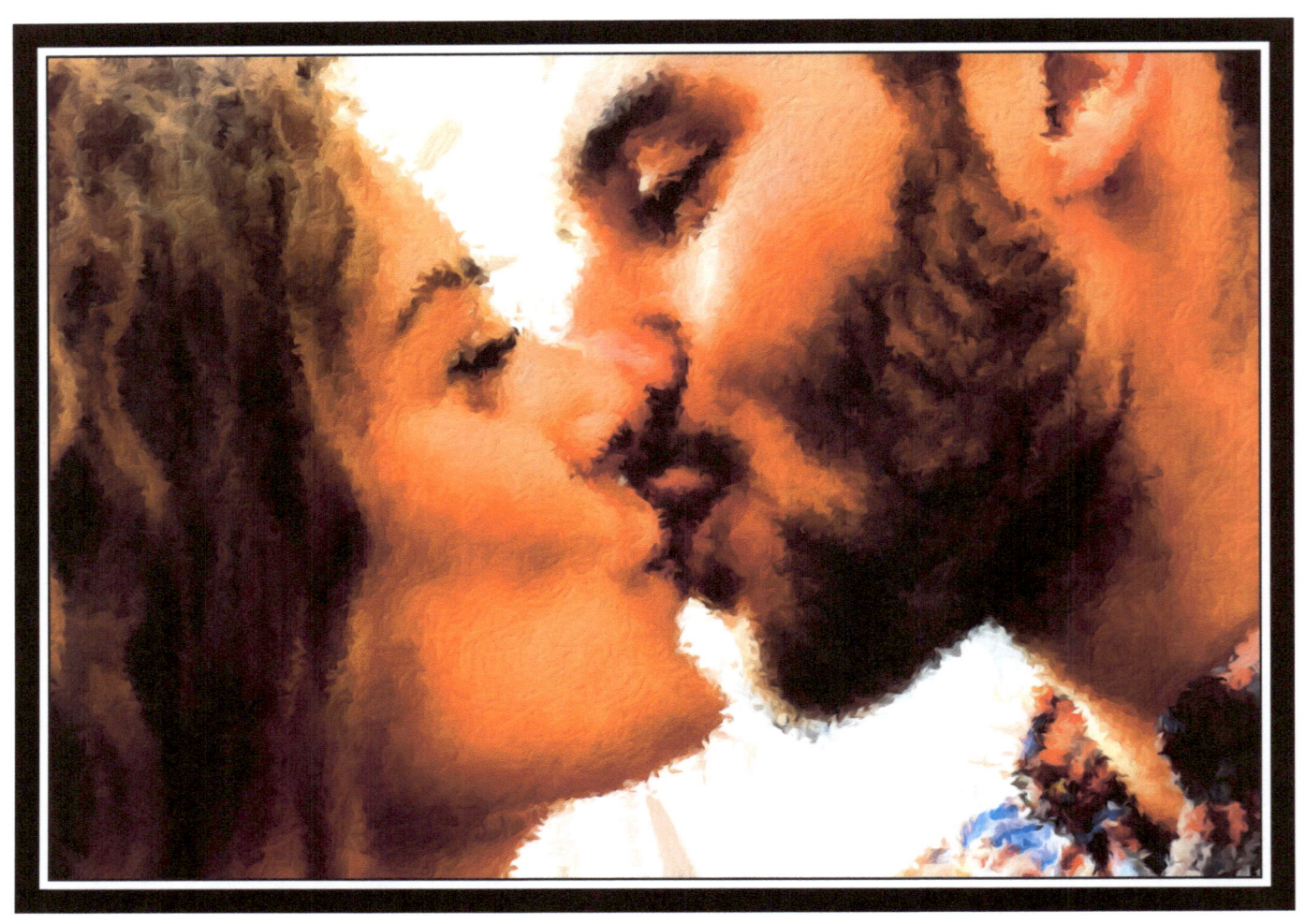

The kiss - Picture in the middle

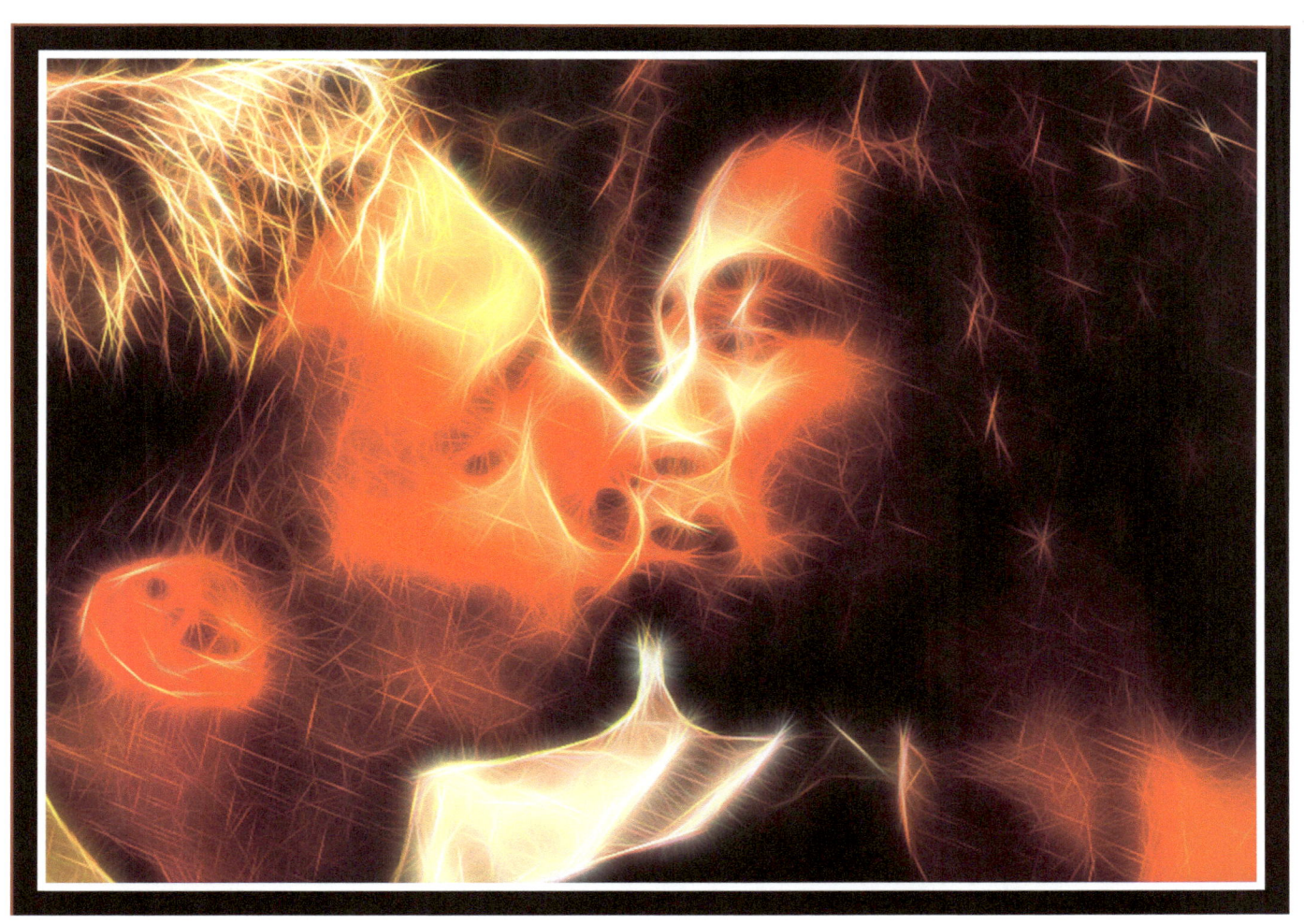

The kiss - Picture on the right

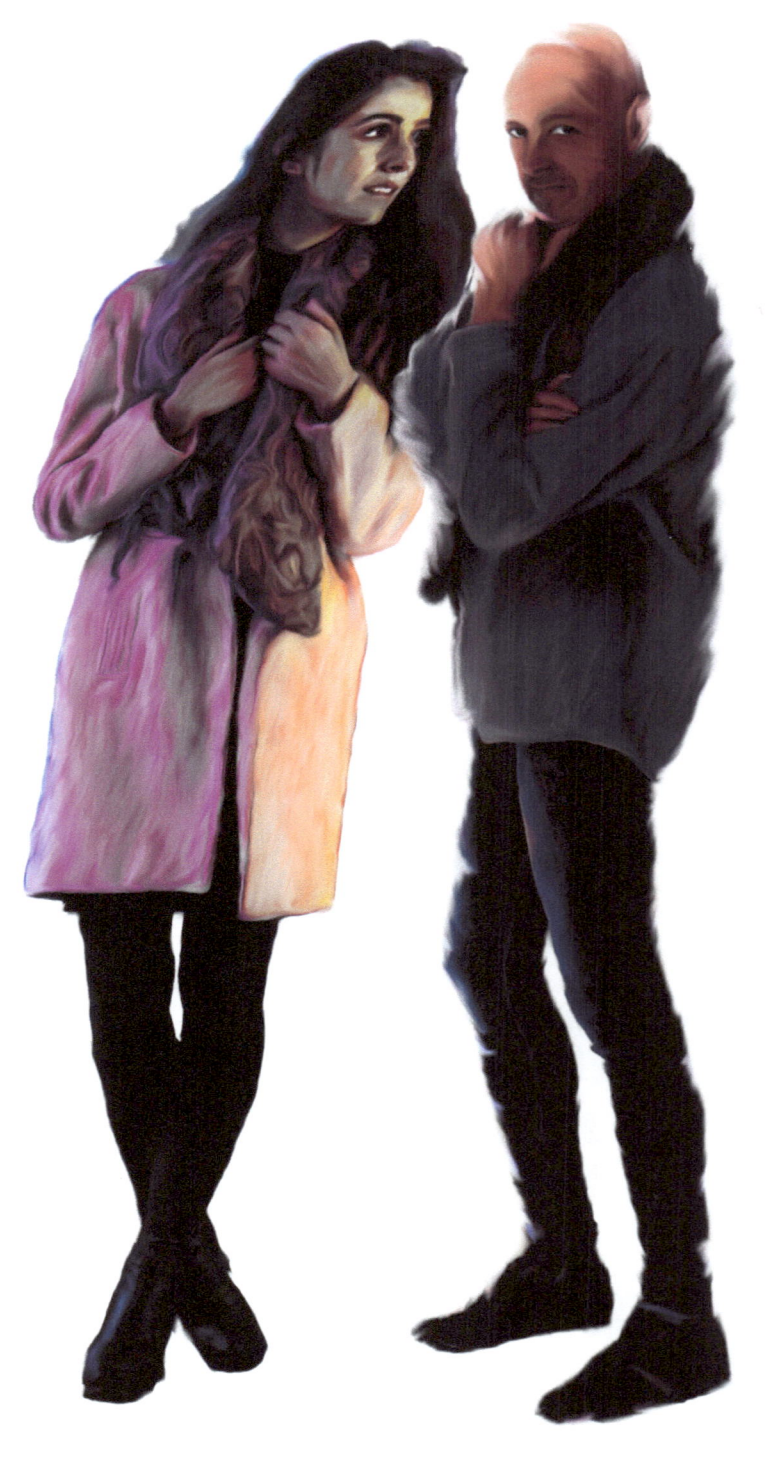

The kiss – A man, a woman

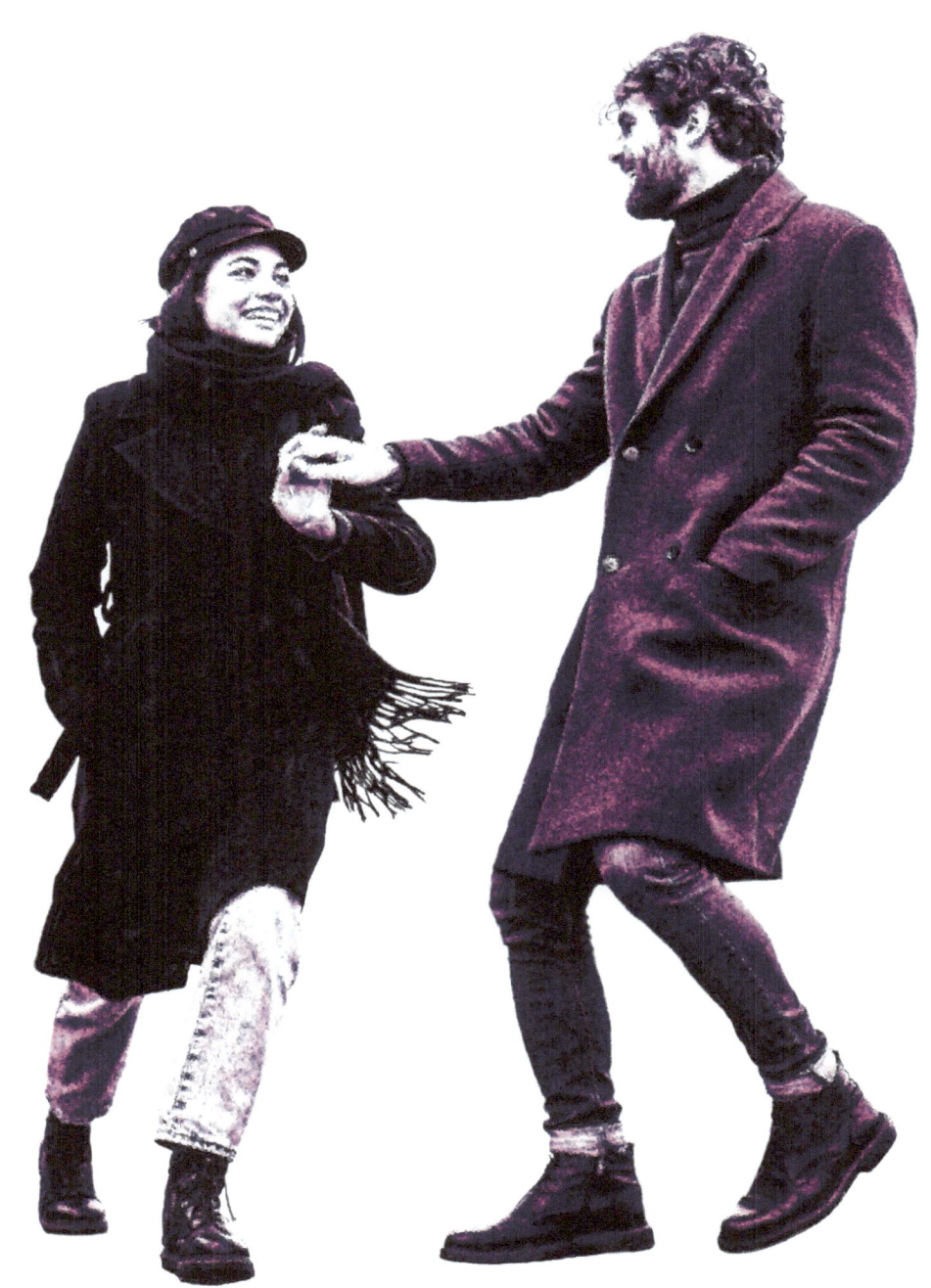

The kiss - The couple